Parole and the Community Based Treatment of Offenders in Japan and The United States

Parole and the Community Based Treatment of Offenders in Japan and The United States

L. Craig Parker, Jr., Ph.D.

UNIVERSITY OF NEW HAVEN PRESS

Contents

Parole and the
Community Based Treatment
of Offenders in Japan and
The United States

Preface

During the period of my Fulbright research in Japan on the police in 1980-81, I had the good fortune of meeting Ken Hatttori, a Japanese probation officer. Assigned to the Tokyo Family Court, he and I developed a friendship and got together on a number of occasions. While I was not addressing issues in the field of corrections or parole at that time, Ken was helpful in arranging a visit to a psychiatric hospital for adolescents and a local prison. We had a number of discussions about the nature of probation and parole in Japan.

Later, in 1983, when I decided to embark on this study of parole and the community based treatment of offenders I contacted him to ask for his assistance. It was through his willingness to introduce me to top ranking officials in the Rehabilitation Bureau of the Ministry of Justice that allowed this project to move ahead. As many Americans who have endeavored to do research in Japan know only too well, a "go-between" is essential. The Japanese word for this is *nemawashi*, "to lay the groundwork for obtaining one's objective." As one of my Japanese scholar friends once remarked, "Craig, you don't pick up the phone and get things done here the way you do in the United States." Indeed, personal introductions are a critical ingredient in initiating a project.

I would like to thank a number of other persons who were particularly helpful in my undertaking this research. At the Rehabilitation Bureau's main office in Tokyo both Kakissawa-san and Suzuki-san were helpful in the initial planning and arranging of interviews. They responded to all of my requests and I was denied nothing. There were many other probation officers and staff of half-way houses throughout Japan, including those in Tokyo, Kofu, Chiba and Kyoto that were helpful and generous with their time. Invariably they responded in a friendly and frank manner during my interviews and visits.

In the United States, Chris Scriabine was extremely helpful in offering her advice in my rewriting major portions of the manuscript. My friend and colleague Lynn Monahan also offered her criticisms of the first draft of the manuscript. Both Lawrence and

Virginia Parker, as they have so often done in the past, offered useful comments. My friend, Jennifer Newton of Guilford, Connecticut designed the cover for the book.

My editor at the University of New Haven Press, Professor Tom Katsaros, has been very helpful and I feel indebted to him for moving the process along so quickly. Candy Ruck did a marvelous job in typing several drafts of the manuscript and her assistance was appreciated. Finally, I would like to thank the W.R. Grace Company for providing me with a Summer Research Fellowship that allowed me the time to write up the data collected in Japan in 1983. The University of New Haven also provided travel and expense support during the field study in 1983. Dean Bill Gere of the Universty of New Haven's Graduate School has continued to be supportive of my research activities as has Dean M.L. McLaughlin of the School of Business.

While I feel indebted to all of the above mentioned parties for their assistance, any remaining difficulties of form or content are, of course, my own.

L. Craig Parker
Professor, Department
of Public Management
University of New Haven
June 1986

CHAPTER I

Introduction

IT IS NO longer fashionable to talk about rehabilitating offenders in America because criminal justice experts have encouraged the public to believe it is an impossible task. Therefore, society has decided to put offenders behind bars as fast as judges can mete out sentences, and this process is linked to one of the highest prison rates in the world. The United States currently has a prison rate of 177 per 100,000 population with 432,829 individuals incarcerated—the highest level ever recorded (Taylor, 1983).

Contrast those figures with those of Japan in which just 35 persons per 100,000 were imprisoned and the overall prison population was only 42,580 (Clifford, 1983). Keeping in mind the fact that Japan's total population of 119 million is approximately half that of the United States, these are impressive differences. One reason the prison population is much less in Japan is because sentences are much shorter—fewer than four percent of prisoners are sentenced for longer than three years, while in the United States, 80 percent of those in state institutions are sentenced for five years or longer (Webb, 1984). How does Japan deal with criminal offenders? Do they emphasize goals of punishment or rehabilitation? Regardless of their priorities, are they engaged in programs that merit our consideration?

Although the imprisonment of criminals achieves the short-term societal goal of removing them from our streets, the very large majority will eventually return to their communities. Most Americans seem to forget that fact as they pressure their legislators for longer sentences. Complicating matters is the fact that some types of offenders, including dangerous ones, commit more than their share of offenses (Moore, Estrich, McGillis & Spelman, 1985). It is these violent chronic offenders, in the eyes of some policy makers, that should be incapacitated or taken off the streets.

1

On the other hand, how can we ignore the fact that incarceration clearly has a profoundly destructive impact on prisoners' lives and personalities? Some have suggested that we do so at our own peril, as these individuals, upon their return to their communities are often more inclined to commit crimes and atrocities. Of course this debate is not a new one; it's been raging for many years.

Do we punish, rehabilitate, or warehouse offenders? Often, our response has been mixed in terms of goals. Sometimes it appears we are attempting to accomplish a little of each, usually with disastrous results. Regardless of our objectives in confining offenders, there are many who believe prison is a destructive experience. This view of incarceration has been repeatedly documented by scholars, government officials, newspaper reporters, and even criminals themselves. Jack Abbott, a convicted murderer and self-educated writer befriended by Norman Mailer, vividly recounted his many years of incarceration in which the cruelties imbedded in the system were illuminated in excruciating detail (Abbott, 1981). Abbott was paroled shortly after the publication of his searing work, only to murder again within weeks of his release. Nonetheless, the validity of his analysis of prison conditions goes unchallenged. Goffman's (1961) work on *Asylums* helped to elucidate the destructiveness inherent in a variety of institutional settings, and presented the common theme that runs the gamut from mental hospitals to correctional institutions.

⌈One of the most vexing problems faced by justice authorities in both Japan and the United States is deciding who to release back into the community on parole. The potential dangerousness of a released offender is a critical consideration, yet the ability to assess dangerousness (including those hospitalized in so called hospitals for the "criminally insane") has remained elusive. Regardless of the screening devices employed (e.g. psychiatric interviews, psychological tests, extensive case histories, etc.), researchers have been unable to develop a method that has proved valid and reliable.⌋

Overall, the problem of identifying offenders capable of adjusting to the community has seemed intractable. A study by Werner (1985) found that 28 percent of those who entered prison in 1979 would still have beeen in jail if they had served the maximum term to which they were sentenced.

Upon the occasion of being appointed Commissioner of New York City's Department of Corrections, Jacqueline McMickens, a veteran officer with 19 years of experience, offered her views on the crisis atmosphere of the city's system: "When you're overcrowded, when you herd a large number of people together, you spend a lot of time just stopping fights. We're charged with custody and control, and *caring* (author's italics) gets back at the back end of that. You can only do so much in eight hours" (Mydans, 1984, p. B 6). Later in an interview with *The New York Times* reporter, she stated an even stronger opinion concerning the prospects of rehabilitation within prison, "Jail must be a really wasted experience for a lot of people. You can't rehabilitate them. I don't think that's something you can do in a jail" (p. B 6).

Unquestionably, many projects designed to assist incarcerated and released offenders have met with failure, but a few efforts provided encouraging results, according to Martinson and Wilks (1976). Their work was considered a landmark and widely hailed, primarily by critics of the system. They studied a great variety of programs that included smaller caseloads on probation or parole, intensive supervision of caseloads, early release from confinement, group therapies of various kinds, halfway houses, pre-release centers, and the use of tranquilizing drugs (Martinson, 1976). While the dismal results of most of the programs surveyed were headline news on the CBS "60 Minutes" television program, the handful of projects that had demonstrated positive results were virutally ignored. Thus, Martinson's work has most often been cited by those who argue that rehabilitation does not work. In turn, this has contributed to the widespread public view that we should "lock 'em up and throw away the key."

Nevertheless, approached from a different perspective, our society still has many good reasons for attempting to identify those programs and efforts that produce positive results. Even ignoring the liberal, humanitarian concerns of those like the American Friends Service Committee, who argue compellingly for better treatment of offenders, there are very sound economic reasons for treating offenders in communities as opposed to incarcerating them in prisons. Any program that can reduce recidivism, whether it includes confinement or not, should be worthy of our consideration.

The cost of incarcerating offenders has skyrocketed in both Japan and the United States in recent years. While costs vary from state to state, the cost of imprisoning an offender in the United States is now well over $10,000 per year (Taylor, 1983).

As already noted, while many justice scholars and government officials have abandoned hope of finding approaches that work, for some the search continues. Not that there is necessarily any one, single model or type of program that can be found that works. That type of search is undoubtedly destined to be illusory. Rather, it may be that we should pin our hopes on developing rehabilitation models that incorporate the best features of presently existing programs and at the same time selectively incarcerate truly incorrigible dangerous offenders.

The Purpose of This Research

The author's approach to the problem has led to examining what Japan is doing in this field. After an earlier study on the Japanese police system (Parker, 1984) completed under a Fulbright Fellowship, the foundation was already in place to pursue the present study of community based programs for released offenders. The subject of the Japanese police had already attracted the interest of David Bayley (*Forces of Order: Police Behavior in Japan and the United States*, 1976) and Walter Ames (*Police and Community in Japan*, 1980). However, no Western scholar had attempted a major field study of Japan's policies and programs for released offenders. *Therefore, the main purpose of this study is to provide a descriptive overview of Japan's services in the field of offender rehabilitation and to offer comparisons with the United States' approach.*

This study has an anthropological flavor, as it relies on interviews, observations, and visits in the field. Interviews were conducted with probation officials, volunteers, parole board members, legal scholars, halfway house "residents" and private citizens in various parts of Japan including Toyko, Chiba, Yokohama, Kofu, and Kyoto. To buttress the field investigation, and to supplement that portion of the study, various articles and research reports by Japanese scholars were included in the analysis. These are materials that are drawn upon for the first time by a Western scholar for publication in an English language book. The approach of this study is a broad one. It is designed to lay the foundation for more narrowly focused work in the future. Therefore, the intent has been to paint the larger landscape as opposed to seizing on limited problems and issues.

Unquestionably, there is a great need in Japan for sharply focused, well designed experimental studies in the field of offender rehabilitation that will help to answer important policy questions. The type of study that would allow one group of released offenders to be treated by method "X", while a similar group is exposed to method "Y", would help to shed light on what works. Programs along these lines that should be evaluated include the principal ones such as parole, the large scale use of volunteers, and halfway house efforts. Yet, little experimentation in the field of offender rehabilitation is going on at this time in Japan. The United States is more active in this regard with both private and public agencies involved. Organizations like the Vera Institute for Justice in New York City, the Safer Foundation, the United States Department of Justice, and a variety of ex-offender groups, to name just a few, are continuing to explore alternatives to incarceration. While these efforts are on a smaller scale than they were ten years ago, as a result of our preoccupation with punishing offenders, we continue to be more experimental and have engaged in a greater variety of approaches than the Japanese.

In both nations, however, many projects are not adequately researched so that decisions can be made concerning their effectiveness. Research and experimentation in any field is often spurred by a sense of urgency or crisis. That condition, or at least the perception of it does not exist in Japan. True enough, newspaper articles continue to alarm the Japanese public wth their descriptions of escalating rates of juvenile delinquency, but the public is not treated to the daily doses of sensationalized lurid crime reporting that is so common in the media in the United States. Even when the Japanese public is aroused by a particular increase in criminal activity, as is the case of the concern wth juvenile delinquency, it is police budgets that benefit not budgets that supervise released offenders, such as the Rehabilitation Bureau's. A senior probation official, Takahashi-san, of the Kyoto Probation Office citing an historical incident, noted that many years earlier a parolee had killed a socialist leader by the name of Asananu and immediately thereafter the government had added 100 new parole officers.

But he explained "more often our work goes so smoothly that the government sees no need to increase our budget."

Recidivism

Another factor that might be used to encourage greater innovation and spur research is recidivism rates. Recidivism rates, of course, refer to the number of times a person recommits criminal offenses. Rates are somewhat lower in Japan than in the United States, but at 50 percent they are still very costly (in both human and economic terms) for the Japanese (Webb, 1984).

One study of recidivism in the United States noted that of 255,936 persons arrested between 1970 and 1975, 164,295 had been arrested previously at least once resulting in a rate of 64.2 percent (Federal Bureau of Investigation, 1976). The recidivism rates for automobile theft and robbery were particularly high—78.8 percent and 77.6 percent respectively for the same five year period (1970-1975). Data for the exact same period in Japan are not available, but the following statistics have been published by Japan's Ministry of Justice (National Statement of Japan, 1980). For the five year period from 1957 to 1962, 62.3 percent of all discharged offenders were recidivists, while the percent declined to 58.2 percent for the five year period after 1973. Thus, the rate at which criminals repeat offenses in Japan and the United States for the period of the early to mid-1970's appears somewhat higher in the United States. Data for 1981 for U.S. state prisons and Japanese prisons were 64 percent and 50 percent respectively (Webb, 1984).

Finally, data reported by the Bureau of Justice Stastistics, an agency of the U.S. Department of Justice, revealed that 84 percent of arriving inmates at state prisons around America in 1979 were repeat offenders (Werner, 1985). The research indicated that 61 percent had previously been imprisoned. It further noted that about 60 percent of those who will return to prison in 20 years will do so within the first three years.

As noted earlier, the recently published work by Moore, Estrich, McGillis & Spelmen, (1984) stated that a relatively small number of all offenders are both dangerous and chronic in their criminal patterns. Specifically, the researchers found that 5 percent of criminal offenders accounted for half of the violent crime in the United States. Furthermore, 1 percent of offenders committed more than fifty serious offenses per year.⌋

By contrast, there are many fewer dangerous offenders in Japan, For example, in Tokyo there were just 169 homicides committed in 1982 while roughly ten times that number were committed in New York City, a slightly less populated city. Just 502 robberies were committed in Tokyo during 1982. Roughly 225 times as many robberies were committed in New York City during the same period. (More extensive data on Japanese crime rates is provided in Tables 1 and 2 in Chapter 3). The ratios of crime are comparable for the two countries on a nationwide basis.

Given the fact that there are many more dangerous offenders in U.S. prisons, the task of rehabilitation becomes a very different one. In both countries justice officials concentrate this effort in the post-release period. Few United States prison wardens would make any claim that their charges are rehabilitated during the period of confinement. On the other hand, Japanese prison authorities believe that some offenders may repent during this period of incarceration and be able to profit from prison programs. Again, recidivism data may be viewed as modest support for their optimism. Incidentally, there were no prison murders in Japan in 1981, but there were 91 in the United States (Webb, 1984).

Comparing the effectiveness of programs and policies designed to rehabilitate released offenders in Japan and the United States is very difficult. In addition to vast cultural differences, there are different social attitudes towards crime, different systems of reporting criminal offenses, along with different vehicles created to process offenders upon their release.

In Japan, as the United States, there is a strong community resistance to helping released offenders. The stigma remains strong in both countries, but it appears more powerful in Japan. Citizens in both countries are unwilling to provide job training, employment opportunities and decent housing for ex-offenders. Japanese citizens, like their American counterparts, resent their taxes being spent on prison construction. The understandable anger and frustration with criminals and their victims has resulted in a short sighted perspective. Even for conservatives who favor greater punishment and longer sentences, they must face the fact (as well as the rest of us) that once an offender is released it's in everyone's best interest that he succeed.

In summary, while general statistical data on recidivism rates are not dramatically different for Japan and the United States, the task is quite different in each nation. The Japanese are faced with a much lower crime rate and fewer violent offenders. Sentences are longer in the United States and the incarceration rate per 100,000 population is one of the highest in the world. The United States, however, exhibits a more experimental approach in attempting to rehabilitate offenders.

REFERENCES

Abbott, J. *In the Belly of the Beast*. New York: Random House, 1981.

American Friends Service Committee. *Struggle For Justice*. New York: Hill & Wang, 1971.

Clifford, W. "Crime and Prison Punishment: Some Facts and Figures." *The Japan Times*, Sunday, July 17, 1983, p. 14.

Federal Bureau of Investigation *Uniform Crime Reports*. Washington, D.C.: U.S. Superintendent of Documents, 1976.

Goffman, I. *Asylums: Essays on the Social Situation of Mental Patients and Other Inmates*. Garden City, New York: Anchor Books, 1961.

Greer, W. "Ex-Convicts Fault Justice System; Contend It Fails Inmates." *The New York Times*, Saturday, February 25, 1984, p. 27.

Koschmann, V. *Authority and the Individual in Japan*. Tokyo: University of Tokyo Press, 1978.

Martinson, R. "Viewpoint on Rehabilitation." In R. Carter and L. Wilkins *Probation, Parole, and Community Corrections*. New York and London: John Wiley & Sons, Inc., 1976, pgs. 40-44.

Martinson, R., Lipton, J., and Wilks, J. *The Effectiveness of Correctional Treatment*. New York: Praeger, 1976.

Mitchell, R. *Thought Control in Pre-War Japan*. Ithaca, New York: Cornell Universty Press, 1976.

Moore, M., Estrich, S., McGillis, D., and Spelman, W. *Dangerous Offenders: The Elusive Target of Justice*, Cambridge, Mass.: Harvard University Press, 1984.

Mydans, M. "Official With a Mission—Jacqueline Montgomery McMickens." *The New York Times*, Thursday, January 19, 1984, p. B6.

Nakane, C. *Japanese Society*. Berkeley: University of California Press, 1970.

Parker, L. "What the U.S. Can Do To Lessen Crime—Copy Japan." *The Japan Times*, January 18, 1981, Op-Ed page.

Parker, L. *The Japanese Police System Today: An American Perspective*. Tokyo, Japan: Kodansha International/Harper & Row, 1984.

Taylor, S. "Strict Penalty for Criminals: Pendulum of Feeling Swings." *The New York Times*, Tuesday, December 13, 1983, p. A1.

Webb, J. "What We Can Learn From Japan's Prisons." *Parade Magazine*, January 15, 1984, p. 7.
Werner, L. M. "84% Repeat Offender Rate Examined." *The New York Times*, Monday, March 4, 1985, p. 22.

CHAPTER II

The Japanese Culture
and Low Crime Rates

BEFORE EXPLORING JAPANESE programs for released offenders, a few words about the nature of Japanese society and its relationship to low crime rates seem appropriate. Knowing something about Japanese culture is essential for appreciating how their community based programs for offenders operate.

One of the most important works on Japanese society is the work of Nakane (1970). She noted that the most characteristic feature of Japanese society was "the single bond in social relationships: an individual or a group has always one single distinctive relation to the other. The working of this kind of relationship meets the unique structure of Japanese society as a whole, which contrasts to that of caste or class societies. And the Japanese values are accordingly manifested" (Nakane, 1970, p. X). She went on to state that groups, which are so pervasively important throughout Japanese society, might be identified by applying two criteria. One criteria was the individual's common *attribute*, the other the situational position in a given *frame*. An attribute might refer to a specific occupation or profession. It might be acquired not only by birth but by achievement. Frame is more circumstantial or the context. The group consciousness of the Japanese relies considerably upon the frame, whereas in the United States the attribute is more important and prominent. This emphasis upon frame in Japan is reflected in the fact that when a Japanese "faces outward", as Nakane states, and "affixes some position to himself socially he is inclined to give precedence to institution over kind of occupation" (p. 3). Therefore, instead of saying he is a psychologist when introduced, he will first offer his university, because that is primary. For example, he will state that he is a faculty member at Tokyo University and secondarily offer that he is a psychologist. When a man says he is from Toyota, one may imagine him to be an engineer or salesman, but in fact he may be a janitor. Among intellectuals, what matters most socially is not whether a person holds or does not hold a Ph.D. but rather from which university he or she graduated. Thus, the criteria by which Japanese classify individuals is the particular institution or frame rather than the universal attribute.

The manner in which group consciousness works is also revealed in the way Japanese use the term *uchi* (house) to mean the place of work, school, office, or business to which one belongs. There frequently is a feeling or sense of family as it applies to one's co-workers or schoolmates. As many Americans are now aware, Japanese corporate heads and officials treat their underlings in a paternalistic benevolent way in Japan. The notion of lifetime employment is related to relations among workers, executives and owners. Workers go on holidays together, and the boss may act as a go-between in arranging one's marriage. Although, let me hasten to add, arranged marriages offer far more choice to the potential partners than they did in earlier times. In modern Japan it is more a matter of setting up the initial introduction. The notion of *uchi* also extends to relationships with one's neighbors in a small town. Those relationships may be more important than with relatives who live some distance away. As Nakane states, "You can carry on your life without cousins, but not without your neighbors" (p. 7).

People with different attributes, let's say an accountant and chauffeur employed by Honda, can be led to feel that they are members of the same group and that the feeling is strengthened by a "we" versus "they" feeling. For example, in competition for market share it's Honda versus Nissan, Toyota, and Mazda, etc.

In Japan, consensus and agreement on decisions is characteristic of group behavior. Sometimes Japanese have to consult their companions over the most trivial matters imaginable. One time while the author was on a weekend expedition to the Mt. Fuji area, and was bicycling around a nearby lake, a friend was asked to stop for a cup of coffee at a roadside stand. Amazingly enough, all fifteen cyclists were stopped and gathered together before a decision was reached. Japanese call a conference over the slightest thing and more than once American businessmen have felt impatience at the snails pace of Japanese decision making. It seems like it will take forever to get an answer to a question!

Another reflection of the cohesiveness that develops among group members and the "me" versus "they" attitude is the distance or coolness toward individuals outside of the group. While a man may shove a stranger out of the way to get a seat on a subway, the same person will act deferentially and with courtesy toward a member of his own organization, particularly if that party is a superior. The same attitude of a group may extend to a broader indentification with fellow Japanese generally and is reflected in attitudes toward minority group members such as Koreans or outcasts such as *burakumin*. (See for example, Mitchell's *The Korean Minority in Japan*.) This matter of discrimination will be discussed at greater length later in this chapter.

To summarize, group activity, group affiliations, and human relations are exclusively one-to-one. Typically, a single loyalty prevails. Of course, one may be a member of several groups, but in those instances one group is preferred and stands above the others. In contrast, individuality, so highly prized in America, is viewed as selfish by Japanese standards. The individual identifies with the group and seeks his fulfillment through working and socializing with his fellows.

The large network of both formal and informal groups has implications for the criminal justice system. The social fabric is more tightly woven in Japan. In studying the police system in 1980–81, the author was surprised to discover the large number of crime prevention associations, both local and regional, that assist law enforcement authorities.

In considering a society characterized by groups, one must include the nature of Japanese family life. Families are far more cohesive than in America and there are far fewer divorces. While divorce rates are increasing in Japan, in 1978 there were only 1.14 cases per 1,000 population while in the United States the rate was 5.2 per 1,000 for the same year (Murata, 1981; U.S. Bureau of Census, 1980). Japanese family members have a sense of responsibility and obligation for one another that appears to provide strong emotional support for the individual. By the same token, many Japanese feel a strong sense of shame and embarassment if a family member were to commit a criminal offense, or otherwise behave in a manner which would reflect dishonor upon the family.

Another critical factor in Japanese society is the way in which relationships are organized, both in terms of vertical and horizontal features (Nakane, 1970). The vertical feature is more important than in the United States. The notion of ranking also enters this equation. It is surprising for an American to learn how delicate rankings are in all walks of life, whether it comes to ranking the prestige of steel companies or elementary schools. Rankings are often based on seniority (i.e. date of appointment), relative age, etc. They can be found in the arts as well as in business, government, and university life. They certainly exist among police, judges, and probation officers in the criminal justice system. They are manifested in formal introductions and the use of language used in the initial meetings. One's status is carefully determined as the *meishi* (name card) is presented with both parties bowing to one another. If appropriate, honorifics may be used and Japanese language is intricate enough to allow a variety of speech patterns to cover these circumstances. Rank and seniority frequently overpower merit as Nakane observes:

> In Japan once rank is established on the basis of seniority, it is applied to all circumstances, and to an extent controls social life and individual activity. Seniority and merit are the principal criteria for the establishment of a social order; every society employs these criteria, although the weight given to each may differ accordingly to social circumstances. In the West, merit is given considerable importance, while in Japan the balance goes the other way. (p. 29)

Age, popularity, sex, and status are all important in fixing the social order, but status is clearly more important. Status is important in social discourse and in doing the police research, as well as in undertaking the current study, the researcher frequently encountered the problem that when he chose to interview a number of police officers or probation officials only the senior most person spoke among the group. Status is reflected in the classroom whereby the teacher lectures and the students listen. Rarely are the students engaged in debate and discussion. Visiting Japanese professors have occasionally been disarmed when they've had to contend with American students who are taught to debate and challenge authority.

Junior level individuals take care not to openly confront or challenge senior members. The importance that Japanese attach to social harmony must be recognized. Included are such principles of human behavior as getting along with others and the avoidance of aggression and conflict. The emphasis displayed in greetings, introductions and personal courtesies—including bowing—are part of the elaborate social rituals designed to dampen negative feelings and hostility. As the author noted in an article for *The Japan Times*, "Japanese rarely act on feelings of hostility in public. A shove will not bring retaliation in a physical way or probably even in a verbal way" (Parker, 1981). Christopher (1983) noted that, from a Japanese point of view, the overriding advantage of an indirect approach was that it ruled out the possibility of direct personal conflict. He added:

> The extent to which Japanese dread such conflicts is not always evident from the way in which they deal with Westerners; because they are intellectually aware that in the West confrontation is regarded as healthy and useful, a certain number of Japanese now try to accomodate this strange foreign taste. Their efforts to do so are often enough both forced and inept. . . (p. 54)

Racially and culturally, Japan is one of the most homogeneous societies in the world. Christopher's (1983) comment on this topic is revealing:

> The notion that Japanese can read one another's minds—or at least, faces—simply because they share a common background may at first blush seem improbable. But that is only because outsiders commonly fail to appreciate what a truly extraordinary degree of ethnic and cultural homogeneity prevails in Japan. (p. 45)

Most students of Japanese criminology, including both American and Japanese, have concluded that the homogeneous makeup of Japanese society is the single most important factor in maintaining low crime rates. There are very few minorities in Japan, with 600,000 Koreans representing the largest group. But this number is relatively insignificant compared to the total Japanese population of over 119,000,000. A smaller number of Chinese live on the five islands that make up the Japanese archipelago. One other minority group is referred to as *burakumin*, or "those who live in hamlets." However, the word *burakumin* is just a euphemism for *eta*, the word originally used to describe those outcasts or untouchables who are believed to be "filthy" by standards of Shintoism. Even today, this is still a taboo subject in Japan. The author has Japanese friends who refuse to discuss the topic.

Historically, *burakumin* were grave diggers, butchers, and tanners of leather who occupied low level jobs in Japanese society. Today, reform minded groups claim that discrimination continues and they point to the ghettos that are particularly large in cities like Osaka, where *burakumin* are clustered. One reads reports of blacklisting techniques employed by large Japanese firms and the careful screening of prospective husbands by the future brides' parents. Not surprisingly, this minority group has a higher crime rate than the general population.

In general, however, Japanese society is essentially homogeneous with the people sharing a long history of racial and ethnic similarity, including a continuity in traditions and values. This homogeneousness ccontributes in a major way to the sense of brotherliness that prevails throughout the nation. The insular attitude of Japanese is related to their history. Undoubtedly, it was the isolation factor that contributed to the inbred and insular quality of life. Not since the eighth century A.D. had there been any new elements that penetrated Japanese society. For more than a thousand years, there had been no intrusion of more than a handful of foreigners into Japanese life.

Conformity is one of the most prominent features of Japanese life. Conforming to traditional values becomes intertwined with group life and a famous saying in Japan is "the nail that sticks out will get pounded down." This message is neither lost on children in a classroom setting nor among workers at a Nissan automobile factory. The conformity that prevails throughout Japanese life appears stultifying to a Westerner, but most Japanese do not veer from this established value. Those Japanese who have worked or studied abroad for any period of time often have adjustment problems upon returning to Japan. For example, a businessman who may have become accustomed to the outspokeness of New Yorkers and who learned to assert himself verbally and otherwise in order to survive in the United States may find it difficult to achieve acceptance from fellow Japanese upon returning to the home office in Tokyo. Behavior that is socially rewarded in America may prove alienating in Japan.

Conformity is linked to the group oriented nature of Japanese society. Due to the influence of group ties, people tend to adapt themselves to their group, accepting its viewpoints on specific issues rather than developing their own opinions. Ezra Vogel (1979), author of the popular *Japan As Number One*, stated "Even if a vote is held, the vast majority commonly follow the group position without developing a separate position of their own" (p. 126). Later in noting how conformity plays a role in politics and the press, he commented:

> No one would advocate limiting the variety of views expressed or suppressing stories. It is doubtful, however, that the limits to expression of variant opinion imposed by group cohesiveness still constitute a serious threat to Japanese democracy. The prewar totalitarian state dominated an unsophisticated public that had no choice but to follow blindly a militaristic government because so few of its members had the sophistication to know otherwise or the opportunities to say otherwise. (p. 127)

Japanese at home and at school are taught to fit in. When Japanese are travelling abroad, they sometimes encounter problems. Unlike in their home country where life is dependable and predictable, they are uneasy in a foreign country. Discussing the plight of the Japanese tourist abroad, Taylor (1983) offered this remark:

> In Japan almost everyone can be expected to stick to the rules, and differences with strangers can usually be ironed out without so much as a raised voice. In the rough-and-tumble of America or Southern Europe, behavioral norms may be vague or entirely absent, and the Japanese have trouble shifting for themselves. (p. 112)

As Vogel's (1979) earlier comment indicated, prewar society in Japan was authoritarian in nature. Interestingly enough, part of the legacy of Japan's totalitarian prewar government is the present respect for governmental authority. This embraces the system of law enforcement as well and must be considered as another factor in the nation's low level of crime. Police officers are not viewed with hostility and seen as alien as in the United States.

While General MacArthur and the American occupation force at the end of World War II superimposed a U.S. type of constitution and political structure on Japan, there is still ample evidence of Japan's history of authoritarianism today. The emphasis on central government as opposed to local government is just one dimension of this. Both types of government exist, but a disproportionate amount of power is vested in the national government and its agencies. At the end of World War II, the American occupation authorities broke up the national police system and imposed the highly decentralized system of policing in which every town and city had its own police force that is so familiar in the United States. However, a number of years later, after MacArthur had departed, the Japanese dissatisfaction with the "inefficiency" of this "patchwork" of police forces resulted in their choosing to return to a national police agency which continues to prevail today.

Before World War II, the Peace Preservation Law and other instruments of repression allowed governmental authorities to arrest left-wing activists. The secret police were feared by local citizens; public prosecutors were given vast power. Citizens' rights were almost unheard of and loyalty to the emperor was taught in the schools (Mitchell, 1976; Koschmann, 1978). Therefore, as a carryover from the earliest period, respect for governmental authority is still very strong in Japan despite the democratization of the country that took place after World War II. While the police are no longer feared as they were prior to World War II, the residue of authoritarianism for the most part takes the form of respect.

Japanese society is still a society in which the sense of obligation is strong. Perhaps it is no longer as central as Ruth Benedict (1946) suggested in her classic, *The Chrysanthemum and the Sword*, but it is still a major ingredient in most on-going relationships. There are a variety of words that mean obligation. *Gimu* means an obligation or duty outside of oneself, like following custom, fulfilling obligations to parents, family, company, and country (Halloran, 1969). *Giri* is a more personal obligation to repay a favor or kindness that someone has done for us. Japanese are very conscious of these obligations and occasionally feel overburdened by them. Vogel's work, *Japan's New Middle Class: The Salary Man and His Familly in a Tokyo Suburb* provides an abundance of examples of *giri* relations.

Most Western scholars would agree with Halloran's (1969) statement that the Japanese are an honest people. Of course they have thieves and criminals among their ranks, but for the most part they take pride in being scrupulously honest about money, property and service. It's considered impolite for a Japanese to count his change like Americans are taught to do. There are numerous accounts offered by Westerners in which they left money exposed or returned to pick up a camera left at a restaurant. In conducting the police research, the author was amazed to discover that at the Ginza Police Department there were more objects reported *found* than *lost*. One doubts that this would be the case in a New York City police precinct.

While most Japanese will acknowledge being egotistical, they are also a highly disciplined people—which indirectly has implications for the low crime rate. This attitude, along with the work ethic, contributed to the so-called "economic miracle" but it also helps to preserve order in the society. Discipline is also linked to the sense of morality in Japan. As Halloran (1969) noted, Japanese morality comes from outside the individual, not from inside. Japanese are not religious in the sense of the Judaeo-Christian Heritage, but they do have a strong sense of social ethics as to what is expected of them. These are more like rules imposed by society. Japanese tend to think of what is proper and improper and what is acceptable or unacceptable to the people around them. Their view of mankind emerges from Confucian teaching according to Halloran (1969). He states, "five relationships determine much of the social order: superior and inferior, father and son, elder brother and younger brother, husband and wife, and friend and friend" (p. 223).

A specific factor related to low crime rates in Japan is the infrequent use of firearms in criminal activity. There are strict gun control laws in Japan. In 1979, only 171 crimes were committed with guns. In the study of the Japanese police system, approximately 50 patrole officers were interviewed in Tokyo before one was found who acknowledged ever having had to draw his weapon. In that particular instance, the officer responded to a bank robbery in progress and had been notified by a supervisor that the person might be armed. Even in that case, the officer was not required to fire his weapon. One police official of the Tokyo Metropolitan Police Department noted that in recent years usually less than 2 percent of all homicides in the Tokyo area involved guns.

In very sharp contrast, in the United States handguns are a major factor in crime! The difference between the two countries on this issue is staggering. During 1981, half of all murders, or more than 11,000, were committed with handguns. Additionally, handguns are used in one-third of all robberies and one-third of all rapes. It was estimated that there were between thirty and fifty million handguns in the United States as of 1981 (Wright, Rossi, and Daly, 1983).

Consistent with the emphasis Japanese place on harmonious personal relationships is the fact that the legal system recognizes the value of resolving differences through the use of non-adversarial methods. There is far less litigation in Japan than in the United States, although it seems to be increasng. Japan controls the total number of legal functionaries who enter the system as professionals—only 500 graduate from the Legal Research and Training Institute each year. Consequently, there are only 3 percent as many lawyers in Japan as in the United States. In Japan, you don't pick up the phone to ask for advice on a minor legal problem. Lawyers are not available for that purpose.

Japan's quasi-national system of law enforcement which includes the highly decentralized system of police boxes (*kōban*) scattered throughout the country makes some contribution to maintaining low crime rates. However, as in most democratic societies, the police play a minor role in this process. Japan's police are extremely well trained, organized, efficient and very professional. The fact that they have established their presence in the form of 15,700 boxes or *kōban* provides the nation with neighborhood policing in the truest sense. Citizens have ready access to police no matter where they live. In the cities, this means that a *kōban* is usually nearby, perhaps only two or three blocks away. As noted above, while the police were intimidating and even aroused fear in citizens prior to World War II, they have completely changed this image since that period.

Polls conducted by the Prime Minister's office reveal that most citizens in Japan today have respect and confidence in the police. The police emphasize service and a large portion of their time is spent on non-law enforcement activities such as crime prevention, counseling, and responding to routine inquiries. They often mediate disputes between neighbors.

At the grassroots level of the neighborhood *kōban* , officers engage in extensive foot and bicycle patrol which helps to facilitate contact with local citizens. Officers usually reside in the neighborhood where they work. In the case of rural police boxes (*chuzaishō*), the officer and his family reside in the living area in the rear of the building. The fact that Japanese police, by tradition and not by law, make two annual visits to all households and commercial establishments is further evidence of their integration into the local community. This tradition has gone on for more than a century and while police did not always enjoy the level of acceptance that they now experience, today it is an effective system with excellent communication between police and citizens. Police are careful not to overreach during this "residential survey" and they approach this task by emphasizing their crime prevention role. However, it cannot be denied that if an officer forms a good relationship with a local citizen in his region (officers in *kōban* divide up their district for purposes of these visits), he can learn a great deal about neighborhood activity, including information on various individuals. Because of this highly organized and professionally trained police force, which operates in such a small island country, one must recognize that this undoubtedly helps to maintain a low crime rate.

Economic considerations cannot be ignored. Unemployment rates have tended to be low—around 4 percent during the early 1980's. Combined with general ecomonic affluence is the broad distribution of wealth among all social strata. Thus, Japan possesses a large middle class with a small percentage of individuals on either side of the economic spectrum. Derelicts are not observed as frequently in the streets of Tokyo as they are in New York City.

In summary, values such as interpersonal harmony, discipline, group behavior, conformity, and the importance of family relations play an important part in Japanese society. These are in addition to strict gun control laws, a respect for governmental authority (including the police), a highly efficient neighborhood police system, economic affluence, and a very homogeneous society. Combined, these factors help to explain why Japan enjoys tranquility and a low rate of crime in recent decades.

REFERENCES

Benedict, R. *The Chrysanthemum and the Sword: Patterns of Japanese Culture.* New York: Meridian Books, 1846.
Christopher, R. C. *The Japanese Mind: The Goliath Explained.* New York: Linden Press/Simon & Schuster, 1983.
Halloran, R. *Japan: Images and Realities.* Rutland, Vermont and Tokyo, Japan: Charles E. Tuttle Publishing Co., 1969.

Koschmann, V. *Authority and the Individual in Japan*. Tokyo: University of Tokyo Press, 1978.

Mitchell, R. *The Korean Minority in Japan*, Ithaca, N.Y.: Cornell University Press, 1967.

Mitchell, R. *Thought Control in Pre-War Japan*. Ithaca, N.Y.: Cornell University Press, 1976.

pany, Inc., 1983.

Vogel, E. *Japan As Number One*. Cambridge and London: Harvard University Press, 1979.

Vogel, E. *Japan's New Middle Class: The Salary Man and His Family in a Tokyo Suburb*. Berkeley: University of California Press, 1963.

Wright, J.D., Rossi, P.H., and Daly, K. *Under the Gun: Weapons, Crime, and Violence in America*. New York: Aldine Publishing Co., 1983.

CHAPTER III

A Sketch of The Japanese Justice System

Trends in Criminal Offenses

WHILE JAPANESE GOVERNMENT officials note that crime rates have stayed low generally during the last decade, they express apprehension about the future. They point to the rapid increase in industrialization, rising affluence, the brugeoning of densely populated areas and a "weakening in human values" as factors that they anticipate will contribute to an increase in crime (see Table 1 for a picture of overall crime rates in the last few decades).

There is some evidence to support their concern. A recent newpaper article, citing data published by Japan's National Police Agency, reported that the illegal use of stimulant drugs had increased twenty-six fold over the previous decade. This is the main drug problem, not heroin, cocaine, or marijuana abuse as in the United States. Officials are concerned with the spreading use of this drug among juveniles, housewives, taxi cab drivers, truck drivers and others. The problem, as is the case in the United States, is directly linked to organized crime groups. In Japan, they are called *bōryokudan* or *yakuza*. Justice officials no longer use the latter term as it casts a romantic cloak over these underworld figures.

Organized crime figures continue to bleed Japanese resources, and like their American counterparts, they engage in violent acts—racketeering, extortion, murder, prostitution, and drug smuggling. During 1981, police investigated 52,670 members of organized crime organizations, an increase of 423 from 1980. In 1981, 58.5 percent of the offenders investigated for "intimidation" were gang members, along wth 54.7 percent of Horse Racing Law violators, 53.9 percent of gambling offenders, 49.7 percent of stimulant

TABLE 1
Penal Code Offenses Known to the Police and Penal Code Offenders Investigated by the Police
Source: Japanese Ministry of Justice
Summary of White Paper on Crime, 1982

Year	No. of Offenses Known to the Police		No. of Offenders Investigated by the Police		Population (1,000)	Crime Rate of Nontraffic Penal Code Offenses
	Penal Code Offenses	Nontraffic Penal Code Offenses	Penal Code Offenders	Nontraffic Penal Code Offenders		
1948	1,603,265	1,599,968	539,467	535,918	80,003	2,000
1949	1,603,048	1,597,891	566,943	561,512	81,773	1,954
1950	1,469,662	1,461,044	587,106	578,152	83,200	1,756
1951	1,399,184	1,387,289	586,258	573,909	84,573	1,640
1952	1,395,197	1,377,273	546,986	528,655	85,852	1,604
1953	1,344,482	1,317,141	520,057	492,214	87,033	1,513
1954	1,360,405	1,324,333	513,718	476,992	88,293	1,500
1955	1,478,202	1,435,652	534,060	490,683	89,276	1,608
1956	1,410,411	1,354,102	527,950	470,522	90,259	1,500
1957	1,426,029	1,354,429	544,557	471,600	91,088	1,487
1958	1,440,259	1,353,930	545,272	457,212	92,010	1,472
1959	1,483,258	1,382,792	557,073	454,898	92,973	1,487
1960	1,495,888	1,378,817	561,464	442,527	93,419	1,476
1961	1,530,464	1,400,915	581,314	451,586	94,285	1,486
1962	1,522,480	1,384,784	569,866	430,153	95,178	1,455
1963	1,577,803	1,377,476	606,649	425,473	96,156	1,433
1964	1,609,741	1,385,358	678,522	449,842	97,186	1,425
1965	1,602,430	1,343,625	706,827	440,563	98,275	1,367
1966	1,590,681	1,292,091	740,055	431,324	99,054	1,304
1967	1,603,471	1,217,844	802,578	400,210	100,243	1,215
1968	1,742,479	1,231,886	923,491	391,091	101,408	1,215
1969	1,848,740	1,251,678	999,981	375,132	102,648	1,219
1970	1,932,401	1,277,459	1,073,470	378,023	103,720	1,232
1971	1,875,383	1,242,017	1,026,299	359,267	105,014	1,183
1972	1,818,072	1,221,459	976,692	346,201	107,332	1,138
1973	1,728,726	1,187,936	931,316	354,461	108,710	1,093
1974	1,671,947	1,208,649	852,347	360,365	110,049	1,098
1975	1,673,727	1,232,353	830,128	361,626	111,940	1,101
1976	1,691,229	1,245,766	830,679	357,041	113,086	1,102
1977	1,704,995	1,266,658	822,218	360,865	114,154	1,110
1978	1,776,801	1,335,172	843,295	379,322	115,174	1,159
1979	1,738,407	1,287,879	840,285	366,159	116,133	1,109
1980	1,812,755	1,355,974	869,766	390,194	116,916	1,160
1981	1,925,796	1,462,010	904,609	416,672	117,884	1,240

drug offenders and 44 percent of extortion offenders (Ministry of Justice, 1982). Clearly, organized crime members represent a large portion of the offenders in these categories.

Although the overall number of crimes committed with firearms was just 233 in 1978, 179 of them were committed by *bōryokudan* members. Nonetheless, despite these high percentages of offenses cited by officials, Japanese law enforcement authorities have gained the upper hand in their fight against organized crime in recent decades.

The Japanese Diet (Parliament) enacted several statutory provisions to combat organized crime, including 1958 amendments to the Penal Code prohibiting intimidation of witnesses and unlawful assembly while armed with dangerous weapons, and the 1964 revision of Laws Punishing Acts of Violence. The strict enforcement of these new laws brought about the dissolution of many gangster groups and a reduction in the membership of organizations to 43,303 from over 184,091 at the peak period of 1963. The decline has continued through 1981 and just 2,452 groups were operating that year, with a total membership of around 103,263 (Ministry of Justice, 1982).

Juvenile delinquency represents the second major concern of justice officials. Persons under 20 years of age are classified as juveniles in Japan and they are subject to the special laws and procedures that have been created to cope with their illegal activities. Historically, the number of juvenile suspects investigated by the police peaked in 1951 at 166,433 and then declined for a number of years. In 1964, another peak was reached with 238,830 suspects investigated. The mid-1970's witnessed another decline but by the late 1970's, an increase was again observed with the number reaching 303,915 by 1981. The increasing use of violence in the classroom, with occasional attacks against teachers, has been one of the characteristics of the trend, accompanied by numerous newspaper editorials decrying the upsurge. For example, in February 1983, a group of teenage boys beat up some vagrants in Yokohama—an incident described as "a sadistic orgy" by the English-language *Japan Times*. Three of the victims died.

Another case involved a 14-year old girl in a school in Kisarazu, a community near Tokyo. She was beaten for three hours with a bamboo sword by youngsters from an affluent family who had no previous record of delinquency. In Tokyo, a handicapped teacher stabbed a student with a fruit knife after being harassed and attacked for weeks by a group of boys. *Violent incidents involving junior and senior high school students on school premises totaled 1,961 in 1982, an increase of more than 60 percent from just three years earlier* (Lohr, 1983). Also, the number of incidents of violence against teachers reached 843 for 1982, an increase of four and a half times over 1978, according to the National Police Agency.

Of course, compared with juvenile delinquency rates in the United States the number appears small, but it is the sharp upward trend that causes alarm among the Japanese. The tremendous pressure on young people to succeed academically is considered the main culprit. Interviews the author conducted with counselors at Juvenile Counseling Centers (operated by the Tokyo Metropolitan Police Department) disclosed repeatedly that school pressure was the main cause of juveniles' disruptive behavior.

While the educational system has achieved remarkable success in increasing literacy and technical competence, which in turn has contributed to the economic boom of recent decades, there has been an emotional price to pay. A breakdown in traditional values of discipline and family values has accompanied this rise in delinquency. Critics also point to the rise in Western individualism as a factor in the erosion of cohesiveness of groups. Interviews the author conducted with the police personnel in 1980 strongly support this notion (Parker, 1984). Often it was evidenced in the increasing number of persons questioned by police who cited their right to counsel or other rights. Another reflection of the emotional price paid by adolescents who feel compelled to compete academically is the rash of suicides that occur around exam time—the infamous period of "examination hell" in the Spring of each year. In 1981, 1777 youth under age 24 committed suicide.

Leaving the major twin problems of delinquency and drug abuse in Japan aside, the current data on Tokyo crime rates (Table 2) reveal generally how low the overall crime rate is for one of the world's largest cities. Many of the statistical changes that have occured between 1981 and 1982 may not be indicative of any "real" or ongoing trends. Rather, the numbers may reflect "chance" statistical variations. Of course, where the magnitude of the change is large, there is a greater chance that it reflects a trend. Only subsequent data collection will answer the question. For example, the data cited on "embezzlement" represents a rather sizable leap of 1,582 offenses in one year.

Overall, the category of "felonious offenses" showed a negligible increase in the rate per 100,000 population from 11.4 in 1981 to 12.4 in 1982. This appears to be accounted for by the jump in arson from 230 to 380 offenses. All other felonies show slight reductions for Tokyo from 1981 to 1982.

Dispute Resolution and the Law

Historically, Japanese have been reluctant to rely on formal, legal institutions to resolve disputes. The average Japanese, even today, is not eager to involve himself in a lawsuit if he can avoid it. Rather, the history and tradition of the nation has stressed non-adversarial methods as opposed to confrontational, legal ones for resolving disputes. Japanese legal scholars such as Kawashima (1963) have provided data to support the notion that even when individuals are faced with a serious injury or loss that can be directly attributable to negligence on the part of a company or firm, Japanese are reluctant to sue for damages. Japanese, in shying away from the use of formal, legal means of dispute resolution, prefer to resolve disputes on a more direct, personal level. As Frank Gibney (1975), a noted authority on Japan, stated in his work, *Japan: The Fragile Super Power:*

> To the Japanese, the law is not a norm but a framework for discussion. The good Japanese judge is the man who can arrange and settle the most compromises out of court. When an American calls his lawyer, he is confident and happy to rely on the strength of his whole social sytem, the rule of the law. When a Japanese calls his lawyer, he is sadly admitting that in this case his social system has broken down. (p. 82)

Kawashima's (1963) work stressed that there are two key considerations in Japan:s extrajudicial approach to dispute resolution. First, there is the hierarchical feature where social status is clearly defined in terms of deference to authority. Relationships among family members and friends fit this mold, but even contractual relationships are affected by status. A contract of employment implies the deference of the employee to the employer. Also, the employer can be thought of as cast into a "patriarchal" role as opposed to a "despotic" one. While the employer fulfills the

TABLE 2

Crimes under the Penal Code Offenses and Clearances in Tokyo

Source: Tokyo Metropolitan Police Department Publication, "Kei Shico," 1982—for 1981–1982

Type of Offenses	Offenses Known to the Police		Offense Rate per 100,000 Inhabitants		Clearance		Clearance Rate (percent)	
	1982	1981	1982	1981	1982	1981	1982	1981
Felonious Offenses								
Murder	169	189	1.4	1.6	160	182	95	96
Robbery	502	507	4.3	4.4	352	426	70	84
Arson	385	230	3.3	2.0	292	165	76	72
Rape	388	402	3.3	3.5	332	310	86	77
Total	1,444	1,328	12.4	11.4	1,136	1,083	79	82
Violent Offenses								
Illegal Assembly with Dangerous Weapons	31	62	0.3	0.5	32	61	103	98
Assault	3,582	4,052	30.7	34.9	2,960	3,395	83	84
Bodily Injury	4,248	4,398	36.4	37.9	3,672	3,825	86	87
Bodily Injury Resulting in Death	33	33	0.3	m 0.3	31	32	94	97
Intimidation	369	358	3.2	3.1	4,315	318	85	89
Extortion	1,948	1,788	16.7	15.4	1,461	1,279	75	72
Total	10,211	10,691	87.4	92.2	8,471	8,910	83	83

Intellectual Offenses	Fraud	6,363	6,078	54.5	52.4	4,847	5,044	76	83
	Embezzlement	13,895	12,309	119.0	106.1	14,206	12,540	102	102
	Forgery, Counterfeiting	1,320	1,059	11.3	9.1	1,227	985	93	93
	Bribery	20	14	0.2	0.1	23	15	115	107
	Breach of Trust	29	24	0.2	0.2	29	24	100	100
	Total	21,627	19,484	185.2	168.0	20,332	18,608	94	96
Offenses Against Morality	Gambling	603	438	5.2	3.8	639	469	106	107
	Indecency through Compulsion	674	594	5.8	5.1	345	300	51	51
	Public Indecency, Distribution of Obscene Matters, etc.	690	600	5.9	5.2	542	664	79	111
	Total	1,967	1,632	16.8	14.1	1,526	1,433	78	88
Other Offenses (Except Traffic Negligent Homicide & Injury)	Obstruction of the Performance of Official Duties	683	719	5.8	6.2	680	718	99	100
	Intrusion upon Habitation	2,749	2,874	23.5	24.8	1,377	1,385	50	48
	Destruction	4,954	4,500	42.4	38.8	708	683	14	15
	Others	789	797	6.8	6.9	786	797	99	100
	Total	9,175	8,890	78.6	76.6	3,551	3,583	39	40
Grand Total		256,055	247,184	2,192.5	2,130.9	112,538	110,157	44	45

dominating role in the relationship, he is expected to give in and compromise on requests from the underling. This balance of socially prescribed roles varies from the American system where employers typically are less personal in their contacts with subordinates. Because the "patriarchal" role is not adhered to, American bosses feel little obligation to yield to demands of their underlings.

Historically, a second characteristic of dispute resolution in Japan is that between individuals of equal status, relationships have been both "particularistic" and "functionally diffuse." To elaborate, for members of the same community who are equal in social status, relationships are supposed to be personal (if not intimate) with roles defined vaguely and flexibly to allow adjustment if circumstances dictate. Compromise is the order of the day, if a dispute arises between the parties. One does not anticipate a dispute by drawing up a formal legal contract. However, it must be acknowledged that this tradition has gradually given way to a greater reliance on formal, legal contracts and thus there has been a consequent increase in litigation over the past few decades. Businesses and corporations are still not eager to sue as a *Wall Street Journal* (1981) article noted:

> Japanese companies rarely sue each other, for example over breach of contract; indeed their written contracts usually aren't very specific in the first place. Executives from squabbling companies prefer to work their problems out through personal trust and understanding. Japanese businessmen do not arrive at important conferences wth government officials armed with lawyers. (p. 4)

Also contributing to the reduced level of litigation in Japan is the fact that many matters normally reserved for licensed attorneys in the United States are handled by non-lawyers in Japan. For example, a Japanese undergraduate student who majors in law will be qualified to draft wills, offer tax advice, write contracts and litigate small claims, although he or she will not be identified as a lawyer. Currently, Japan has around 12,000 lawyers serving a population of 119 million people, while the United States has more than 600,000 lawyers offering service to a population approximately twice as large. (Myerson, 1981)

Courts and the Investigation of Crime

As already noted, sentences tend to be shorter in Japan, but trials are often lengthy because Japanese courts seldom hold hearings or trials on a case consecutively. The trial of former Prime Minister Tanaka, who was convicted of taking bribes in the Lockheed scandal, continued for several years before a decision was rendered in 1983.

While having experimented with jury trials for approximately 40 years, Japan did away with them in 1943. During the repressive era before World War II, Japanese were understandably reluctant to serve on juries for fear of offending the sensitivities of prosecutors and judges. Prosecutors even wore judicial robes, further blurring the functions of themselves and judges. Both were employed by the Ministry of Justice. During the post-war period, the courts were reorganized under the independent aegis of the Supreme Court. The present democratic governmental structure, while including the emperor as a figurehead, offers a parliamentary form of government.

In general, Japanese officials cite impressive figures concerning arrest and conviction rates. Confessions are common, and 86 percent of all cases that go to trial include confessions. A bit defensively, officials point out that law enforcement personnel never resort to more than thorough investigations and tough interrogations (Kirk, 1981). But Japanese legal authorities do have some advantages that their American couterparts lack. For example, written evidence can be reviewed by judges and accepted into the trial record. Akio Harada, an official at the Ministry of Justice, stated to the *London Observer's* correspondent (Kirk, 1981):

> In Japan, the written evidence has a big role to play. It's common for witnesses to testify quite differently in court. The court can accept the statement given to the prosecutor, who gathers all the statements he can to support the case. Even if a witness later refused to testify, died or disappeared his statement would still be acceptable to the court. (p. 1)

Public prosecutors defend their 99.7 percent conviction rate by stating that they do not indict until they are virtually sure of winning their cases. They also cite the fact that they often decide not to prosecute many cases of Penal code offenders referred by the police (in 1976, 30 percent were prosecuted). More than 70 percent of those prosecuted were cases disposed of under "summary procedures" during the same year, while the balance were given trials. But most importantly, police and prosecutors can hold a suspect without bail for up to twenty-three days before deciding if there is enough evidence for an indictment.

In general, prosecutors in the United States also have a considerable amount of discretion in their screening of cases. Those that do not warrant prosecution as a result of weak or flawed evidence must be abondoned. Also, for administrative reasons decisions must be made with regard to the limited resources available. Furthermore, cases are weighed with regard to their seriousness (e.g. homicide, robbery, etc.). Moore, Estrich, McGillis, and Spelman (1984) have noted that U.S. prosecutors feel pressured to develop and pursue cases that can be won, so that their conviction rates will remain high. Their statistics on conviction rates tend to support this view. While Japanese prosecutors may claim a 99.7 percent conviction rate, American prosecutors claim a 90.0 percent rate of conviction in which some disposition is reached. However, a substantial number of felony cases received by prosecutors never proceed to disposition. Case attrition is substantial.

In a study funded by the Law Enforcement Assistance Administration, it was found that of all felonies received by prosecutors in 1973, 23 percent were refused prosecution; 30 percent were nolled or dismissed; 2 percent were ignored by the grand jury; 3 percent were found not guilty; 31 percent found or pled guilty, and 12 percent were still open at the end of that year. Thus, while a 90 percent conviction rate sounds impressive it has to be considered in a context in which less than half of the cases proceed to disposition. Furthermore, with the large case attrition that takes place after felony arrests occur, fewer than 15 percent of felony arrests result in felony convictions (Moore, Estrich, McGillis, and Spelman, 1984).

As is the case in the United States, when a person is arrested, he or she must be informed immediately of the reason for the arrest and the right to obtain counsel of his or her own choosing. In addition, the suspect is notified of the right to remain silent.

While the accused is informed of his or her right to retain counsel, some private attorneys who serve as defense counsel complain that they are given very limited time to confer with their clients during the detention period. One private lawyer commented to the author, "The law allows the accused the right to retain defense counsel but in actual practice, this may mean two or three interviews of one hour each maximum—typically only twenty to thirty minutes each during a ten-day period of detention. Even that limited access could be denied if it hampers the ongoing investigation." Often the role of defense counsel is to gain the release of the accused on bail and argue for a reduced or suspended sentence.

In the United States, the role of defense counsel is quite different. American defendants, of course, are entitled to counsel and as criminal defendants are often indigents they receive state supported counsel. Typically, these attorneys are under the public defender system, but in some jurisdictions (such as New York) they are under the umbrella of the legal aid society.

Unlike their colleagues in Japan though, they have a great say in the outcome of their cases. This is primarily because they can engage in plea bargaining, while no such device exists in Japan. While Japanese attorneys are restricted in their access to their clients, American attorneys are given greater opportunities to confer with their clients. However, they are hampered in other ways. Some have as many as 400 cases a year and therefore they cannot adequately spend time preparing a case for trial (Eitzen & Timmer, 1985). Many states provide limited funds to defend the poor and studies have shown that public defenders are typically young and inexperienced. Furthermore, they often graduate from less prestigious law schools, earn less money, and have less prestige as practitioners than those from law firms or corporations (Reid, 1985). Some would have preferred working outside of the criminal law field.

Alternative Dispositions

The flow chart (see Table 3) illustrates that even for the individual who is processed through the early stages of arrest and prosecution, he or she may not be sentenced to prison by the courts. Alternative dispositions are common in Japan. Once the case comes to court, the judges, who frequently sit in panels of three, may fine, acquit, give a suspended execution of sentence, or hand down the latter sentence, "with probationary supervision." The widespread use of these alternative dispositions is reflected in the following data presented to the United Nations Congress on Crime in 1980 (National Statement of Japan, 1980):

Suspension of Prosecution—Prosecutors suspend prosecution for "criminological" reasons (rehabilitative potential of the offender)

TABLE 3
Japanese Criminal Justice System - Flow Chart
Source: Corrections Bureau, Ministry of Justice
1982

Adult

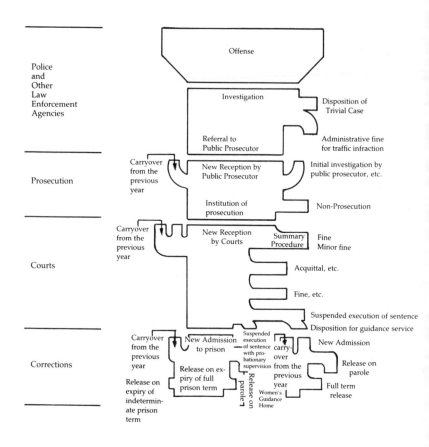

and for reasons related to the security of the community. It is not nonprosecution based on legal or factual deficiences. Of course, as in the United States, it reduces the court load and contributes to the speedy dispositon of other cases. During 1978, suspension was ordered in 212,487 cases of non-traffic law offense, while prosecution was instituted in 531,766 cases for a suspension rate of 28.5 percent.

Administrative Fines for Traffic Violators

Since 1968, Japan has processed the large majority (83.6 percent) of traffic violators (most of which are minor offenses) under the Road Traffic Law. This law allowed violators to avoid the stigma of a criminal conviction and substantially reduced the caseload of the criminal justice system.

Fines

Fines for criminal offenses, as opposed to traffic law violations, are sometimes administered in minor cases. Typically, individuals are fined before a summary court and under this summary procedure can be fined up to 200,000 yen (approximately $834).

Suspended Execution of Sentence

Article 25 of the Japanese penal code allows execution of sentences of imprisonment to be suspended for a period of one to five years under some circumstances; if suspension is not revoked during the specified period for violation of statutory conditions, the sentence loses all legal effect. Typically, "suspension" is considered for defendants who have not previously been incarcerated, or for those who although sentenced to imprisonment at an earlier point have not been resentenced to prison in the previous five year period. It is a powerful tool in the hands of the public prosecutor because it generates serious restrictions on the defendant's conduct. Unlike suspension of prosecution, no new trial is required to imprison a defendant if new violations or offenses occur. Japanese officials have increasingly relied on this technique over the past few decades. From 1960 on, more than half of all convicted offenders of Penal Code offenses have been dealt with in this way. During 1978, it was true of 46,983 persons out of the total of 77,616 imprisoned, for a percentage of 60.5 percent.

Suspended Execution of Sentence with Probation

As noted above, probationary suspension is sometimes a special condition of "suspended execution of sentence." In recent years, probationary suspension has been required of between 17 percent and 18 percent of defendants granted "suspension of execution of sentence." In 1978, 1,837 defendants (3.9 percent of total) were placed under mandatory suspension, while 6,653 (14 percent) were placed in that status through judicial discretion. Probationers who demonstrate progress toward rehabilitation can be provisionally discharged for suspension before expiration of the maximum term of suspension of execution of sentence.

Correctional Institutions

A brief look at the prison system will round out this sketch of Japanese justice. The modern prison system of Japan had its origin in the legislation of the "Kango Kusoku" (Prison Rules) of 1872. According to Clifford (1976), it was patterned after Western style institutions. Not only was the architecture Western, in which penitentiaries housed individual cells, but the criminal codes were Western. In that era, prisons were divided into two jurisdictions—those under the aegis of the central government and those under local municipalities. The Ministry of Justice supervised both. In 1874, the function of prison administraton was turned over to the Ministry of Home Affairs, and later, in 1903, it was taken over once again by the Ministry of Justice where it remains to date. The bureau responsible for administering the prison sytem is now called the Corrections Bureau, while the agency that handles after-care and services for released offenders is termed the Rehabilitation Bureau. These two administrative units, operating under the Ministry of Justice, have a close working realtionship. The Corrections Bureau includes the following categories of institutions: seven detention houses and their 106 branches; 56 prisons and their nine branches and nine juvenile prisons. Four of the prisons are for females, while another four are designated medical prisons, in which emotionally disturbed and medically ill prisoners are treated.

Reports from Americans who have been inprisoned in Japan in recent years suggest a harsh but fair regime imposed by prison officials. One American, Ed Arnett, claimed that he suffered frostbite in his chilly, damp call in Fuchu Prison (Webb, 1984). The Fuchu Prison is reserved for Japan's most serious offenders. Arnett was convicted for possession of two kilograms of marijuana. He stated that during his month-long period of pretrial detention he was interrogated without an attorney and that he eventually signed a confession (written in Japanese) that he could not read. As already noted, Japanese law allows law enforcement officials the right to prevent a suspect from conferring with an attorney if it interferes with the ongoing investigation. Attorneys for defendants argue that frequently it is used for purposes of preventing them from obtaining access to their clients.

Arnett's head was shaved every two weeks, his mail was censored, and he was not allowed writing materials. His diet was similar to that of other Japanese offenders and included seaweed, fish and rice. He was forced to engage in simple manual labor—he made paper bags in his cell—and he was not allowed to look out his window or communicate with fellow prisoners. Furthermore, he was required to endure fourteen months of isolation.

Despite this harsh environment, Arnett told attorney James Webb that he preferred the Japanese system:

> Because it's fair, the Japanese never tried to trick me, even in interrogation. They were always trustworthy. I could have got five years, and they gave me two. The Americans who were helping them wanted me to get 20. The guards at Fuchu were hard, but they never messed with you unless there was a reason. You didn't have to worry about the other prisoners coming after you either. And the laws in Japan are for everybody. That's the main thing. The laws in this country depend on how much you can pay. I'd rather live under a hard system that's fair. (p. 6)

Indeed, abuse and violence within prisons is rare. There were no prison murders in Japan in 1981, but there were 91 recorded in the United States during the same year. In fact, data on assaults, suicides, and homicides wthin Japanese prisons for the period of 1976 through 1981 reveal just a handful of cases (see Table 4).

Officially, Japanese Corrections Bureau policy lists the following disciplinary forms of punishment (Corrections Bureau, 1982):

(1) Reprimand;
(2) Suspension of good treatment for reward for three months or less;
(3) Discontinuation of good treatment for reward;
(4) Prohibition of reading books and seeing pictures during three months or less;
(5) Suspension of work for 10 days or less in the case where the inmate concerned has been permitted on his application to engage in prison labour;
(6) Suspension of using self-furnished clothing and bedding for 15 days or less;
(7) Suspension of self-supply of food for 15 days or less;
(8) Suspension of physical exercise for five days or less;

TABLE 4

Prison Injuries, Deaths, and Escapes, 1976-81

Source: Corrections Bureau, Ministry of Justice, 1982

Year	Escape	Suicide	Fire Incurred	Accidental Death Caused by Negligence in Workshop	Murder or Bodily Injury Against Officers	Murder or Bodily Injury Against Other Inmates	Other Accidental Deaths	Total
1976	5	9			2	1		17
1977	11	15			2			28
1978	6	8				1		15
1979	3	5		1		4	1	14
1980	4	6	1		1	4	1	17
1981	6	4			1	4		15

(9) Whole or partial deprivation of the calculated amount of remuneration for work in prison labour;
(10) Reduction of food for seven days or less;
(11) Minor solitary confinement for disciplinary punishment for two months or less; (p. 19)

Despite some prisoners, like Arnett, being required to engage in meaningless labor, Japanese prison industries are more productive and progressive than those in America. Most offenders, after an initial period of screening and classification, are offered jobs geared to their potential and with an eye toward rehabilitation. Forty thousand offenders were employed in 74 institutins during 1981. Prison industry is organized into three categories: production, vocational training, and maintenance work. Unlike the situation in the United States where unions have lobbied successfully, until recently, to prevent correctional institutions from creating industries that would compete with the private sector, Japanese prison industries have no such restriction. In some prisons, the government provides the raw materials, equipment and facilities, and products are sold on the open market. In others, raw materials, equipment, and facilities are provided by a private contractor who then pays the state the cost of inmate labor. Not unlike the private industry, Japanese prisoners work an eight-hour day, five days a week, with a half-day on Saturday. Table 5 gives a breakdown of the different types of prison work and the revenue generated to the National Treasury. Prisoners are not getting rich in the process. They receive minimal amounts which they are required to save but are then given at the time of release. Some of the funds may be used to buy necessities while at the institution. The average monthly payment was just 2,873 yen (approximately $12 U.S.) during 1981.

One noted authority on Japan's justice system stated, "Japanese prisons are among the best run in the world precisely because they have always been characterized by discipline, industry and a humane concern for inmates" (Clifford, 1984). However, Clifford expressed concern that the historical tranquility of prisons was starting to change with a larger proportion of incarcerated offenders being made up of organized crime members. Not surprisingly, they are less obedient and responsive to the demands of prison authorities. He noted that assaults between inmates increased from 4,685 in 1977 to 5,441 in 1979.

TABLE 5

Categories of Prison Employment and Revenue Generated

Source: Corrections Bureau, Ministry of Justice, 1982

	1982		1981	
	Number of Employed		Amount of Annual Revenue	
Category of Work	Inmates	(%)	(thousand yen)	(%)
Wood-craft	2,326	(5.7)	2,963,439	(17.6)
Printing	1,988	(4.9)	2,297,426	(13.6)
Western-style Tailoring	5,594	(13.7)	2,600,799	(15.4)
Metal-work				
Machinery	3,259	(8.0)	2,635,457	(15.6)
Assembly	4,810	(11.8)	2,106,027	(12.5)
Auto-repairing	152	(0.4)	227,674	(1.4)
Farming & Stockbreeding	283	(0.7)	384,451	(2.3)
Forestry	6	(—)	33,967	(0.2)
Chemical Industry	951	(2.3)	502,851	(3.0)
Paper-making	113	(0.3)	56,263	(0.3)
Paperwork	5,329	(13.0)	646,024	(3.9)
Knitting & Bag-making	473	(1.2)	168,670	(1.0)
Ceramics	182	(0.4)	205,510	(1.2)
Leather-work	1,168	(2.8)	613,741	(3.6)
Spinning	315	(0.8)	154,236	(0.9)
Food-processing	115	(0.3)	38,189	(0.2)
Other Miscellaneous Jobs	3,269	(8.0)	841,496	(5.0)
Jobs Outside Prison	227	(0.5)	223,940	(1.3)
Vocational Training	1,229	(3.0)	165,514	(1.0)
Maintenance Work	7,523	(18.6)	—	(—)
Building & Repairs	1,151	(2.8)	—	(—)
Others	336	(0.8)	—	(—)
Total	40,889	(100.0)	16,865,674	(100.0)

Note: Approximately 160 yen = $1 U.S. Currency

Two brief visits to two prisons in Japan were arranged—Nakano Prison and Hachioji Medical Prison, but frankly there was not adequate time to form much of an opinion. Less than one day was spent at each facility. Both facilities were housed in older buildings, but they were clean and well maintained. Staff were well trained and like so many "things Japanese" organization appeared superb. Correctional staff were trained for a full six months, unlike their counterparts in the United States that often receive four to six weeks of training. Some United States jurisdictions offer just two weeks of training. Japanese correctional officers are kept in good physical condition through required training in martial arts.

Security was tight at the facilities the researcher visited, and as the statistics reveal generally on Japanese correctional institutions, authorities reported no homicides at either institution for the previous year. At Nakano prison, prisoners worked a full eight hour day and received a small compensation for their work. Because of various physical ailments, some prisoners at the Hachioji Medical Prison worked a limited amount or not at all. Prisoners at both institutions function within a spartan regime.

As noted earlier, United States prisons, because of pressure from organized labor, have historically been unable to create productive and useful industrial employment for inmates, but that is changing as private industry begins to offer more correctional services. Also, Chief Justice Warren Burger, United States Supreme Court, has been an outspoken proponent of competitive prison industries. He refers to them as "'factories with walls.''

Since 1983, the Radio Corporation of America (R.C.A.) has operated a juvenile training school for the state of Pennsylvania, and another private company, Behaviorial Systems Southwest, is planning to provide correctional service for arrested illegal aliens in several western states. The Fenton brothers are building a $15 million, 720 bed institution, with workshops, a library, and tall double fences behind an earthworks barricade. Because federal, state and local governments plan on spending as much as $10 billion in 1984 for imprisonment, private businesses are considering the potential for profits by offering correctional services (Krajick, 1984).

Perhaps the most interesting model is the Free Venture approach (Walker, 1985). It is presently operating in Minnesota, Kansas and several other states. The critical General Accounting

Office (GAO) has given the concept a clean bill of health. Inmates work in businesses managed by private entrepreneurs, who are interested in making a profit and inmates are paid competitive wages. Because Free Venture must compete on the open market, it has the same problems that other private businesses have—quality control, productivity, etc. Its purpose is to provide job skills and create good working habits in a modern high-tech industrial environment. So far, one operation is still in business, but two others have gone out of business. As Walker (1985) notes, it's too early to tell if the Free Venture concept will succeed.

In summary, this "sketch" of Japanese justice was offered as a background for understanding their system of probation, parole, and community based programs.

REFERENCES

Clifford, W. *Crime Control in Japan*. Lexington, Massachusetts: Lexington Books, 1976.

Clifford, W. "Doing Time Means Doing Work." *The Japan Times*, February 19, 1984, p. 14.

Corrections Bureau. "Correctional Institutions in Japan." Ministry of Justice, 1982.

Eitzen, D. S. and Timmer, D. A. *Criminology*. New York: John Wiley & Sons, 1985.

Gibney, F. *Japan: The Fragile Super Power*. New York: W. W. Norton & Company, Inc., 1975, p. 82

Kawashima, T. "Dispute Resolution in Contemporary Japan." In *Law in Japan: The Legal Order in a Changing Society*, edited by A. VonMehren, Cambridge, Massachusetts: Harvard University Press, 1963.

Krajick, K. "Private For-Profit Prisons Take Hold in Some States," *The Christian Science Monitor*, Wednesday, April 11, 1984, p. 27.

Kirk, D. "The Shame of Japanese Justice," *London Observer*, February 2, 1981, p. 1.

Lohr, S. "Japan's Classroom: A Budding Blackboard Jungle?" *The New York Times*, March 29, 1983, p. A2.

Ministry of Justice, *Summary of White Paper on Crime 1982*, Tokyo: Research and Training Institute, Ministry of Justice, 1982.

Myerson, A. "Legal Profession in Japan: A Small Guild," *The Asian Wall Street Journal*, February 17, 1981, p. 4.

National Statement of Japan. "Crime Prevention and the Quality of Life," Japanese Ministry of Justice, 1980.

Parker, L. C. *The Japanese Police System Today: An American Perspective*, Tokyo: Kodansha International/Harper & Row, 1984.

Reid, S. T. *Crime and Criminology*, New York: Holt, Rinehart, & Winston, 1985.

Tokyo Metropolitan Police Department. *Keishicho*, Tokyo: Public Relations Division, Metropolitan Police Department, 1982, p. 17. (*Note:* Data in this publication were updated for the author by Japanese Ministry of Justice personnel).

Walker, S. *Sense and Nonsense About Crime: A Policy Guide*, Monterey, California: Brooks/Cole Publishing Company, 1985.

Webb, J. "What We Can Learn From Japan's Prisons." *Parade Magazine*, January 15, 1984, p. 7.

CHAPTER IV

The Organization of Parole and Community Based Services in Japan and America

Brief History - Japan

PROBATION AND PAROLE services in Japan had a very early and rudimentary beginning in the welfare services for poor persons and offenders established by a feudal lord in the latter part of the seventeenth century. Until about the end of the nineteenth century, family ties, and patriarchal control and protection remained very strong. In those days ostracism from the family often forced an individual to drift into vagrancy and even criminal life. However, there was limited opportunity for a discharged offender to integrate himself into the community if he was once accepted by his family upon release. A first time offender, of course, had a better chance of being accepted back by his family, while chronic offenders were often rejected. In the 1880's a case occurred in which a discharged prisoner, rejected by family and community members, was driven to commit suicide (Rehabilitation Bureau, 1981). A philanthropist who was moved by the incident, raised a fund and pioneered in establishing a private aftercare halfway house (known as a Rehabilitation Aid Hostel in Japan) to give shelter, employment and guidance to discharged offenders who had no place to return to in the community. The pioneering efforts of this man, Meizen Kinbara, gave impetus to various religious organizations which founded additional hostels. These early pioneers included Christians and Buddhist priests, some of whom had been prison chaplains. In other cases prison wardens, local politicians and businessmen with strong humanitarian concerns took the lead.

According to Suzuki (1978) it was in 1888 that the Shizuoka Prefecture Exprisoners Aid Corporation (*Schizuoka-Ken Shutsugokunin Hogo Kaisha*) began to accomodate released homeless offenders who lacked jobs. Kinbara's hostel was the first hostel established in the private sector for this prupose. He had been a successful promoter of flood control projects and a manager of an embankment work company. Kinbara had known in advance of the change of policy, and was also informed of the European role of private organizations in the rehabilitation of offenders. In 1880, he established the prison visitors' association, whose paramount aim was to provide moral and religious services for prisoners.

The Penal Code of 1880 provided for the system of conditional release of a prisoner prior to the expiration of his sentence, but in practice it was rarely awarded. Therefore, the scope of services offered by the early hostels was confined to helping ex-offenders who had served out their sentences. None of those services were regulated by government officials at that time.

By 1889, the government's limited program of aftercare was abolished in favor of voluntary and charitable individuals and organizations. This represented, in fact, a financially expedient measure on the part of the government.

General pardons were issued by members of the Imperial Family in 1912 and 1914. The two decrees resulted in a massive total of 36,731 offenders being suddenly released into various communities. This provided further impetus for the government to encourage the private sector to expand aftercare facilities. The early program not only provided discharged offenders with housing, but with counseling and other support services. In 1900, 26 hostels had been created and their numbers grew to more than 100 by 1920. Officials at the Kyoto Probation Office informed the author that services in their region had been initiated by Buddhist priests in around 1900. During that visit to Kyoto, the author met with staff and residents of a halfway house which was supported by funds from a local Buddhist temple. (See Chapter 6 on Halfway Houses)

The introduction of suspended sentences in 1905 along with the increasing use of suspended prosecutions were other factors that stimulated the halfway house movement. The government started to grant subsidies to groups and individuals who ran halfway houses. In 1915, because of World War I, the subsidies were suspended, but the formation of the Offenders' Aid Service Promotion Foundation by Baron Mitsui filled the void during this period. Mitsui was the key person in the famed Mitsui financial group.

In 1939, with the enactment of the Rehabilitation Services Law, two voluntary organizations were created. One was identified as the Rehabilitation Workers Asociation, which preceded the creation of the Volunteer Probation Officers group. The other was the Rehabilitation Service Association which later became the organization serving the current Rehabilitation Aid Hostels. That law required the government to supervise and regulate these facilities and programs.

Decades later, the system was to evolve into the current one in which thousands of government appointed volunteer probation officers offer help to ex-offenders. It wasn't until the 1950's that all elements of a community based rehabilitation system—including probation, parole, and aftercare—were brought together in an integrated fashion.

Brief History - United States

Curiously, it was around the same period—the mid-19th century—when probation and parole started in the United States. The history of these services reflect generally the unsystematic way in which criminal justice agencies emerged. Again, the culprit was the large number of municipal, county, and state jurisdictions.

The history of probation service in the United States can be traced to England. It emerged as a variation on several English practices of the 19th century (McCarthy & McCarthy, 1984). Typically, it took the form of a conditional suspension of punishment pending the offender's good behavior. Judges began to use it as a device to avoid draconian sentences, including the death sentence, associated with minor crimes. The process often involved clergy, judicial reprieval, release on recognizance, and pardon.

Two figures are considered to have been in the forefront of probation in America. The first was Judge Oxenbridge Thacher. He commenced his work in the mid 1800's, and became the first to apply one of the instruments of probation—the use of recognizance. Thacher was a Boston judge who administered it in 1830 in the case of Jerusa Chase (Smykla, 1984). The practice continued and spread to other jurisdictions. The basic idea was simply that as long as an offender abided by the conditions of the court while he was under supervision no further legal sanctions would be applied.

The second figure, whom many consider to be the father of probation in the United States, was John Augustus. Augustus was a Boston shoemaker who initiated probation reform in the police court in 1841. With approval of the courts he was allowed to stand bail for petty offenders and to accept them into custody. He worked without pay. Augustus would appear with the defendant and offer testimony concerning the defendant's behavior and activities in the community. If the person proved industrious and law abiding the charges were dropped (McCarthy & McCarthy, 1984).

An early work quoted one of his experiences (New York Probation Association, 1939):

> In the month of August, 1841, I was in court one morning, when the door communicating with the lock-room was opened and an officer entered, followed by a ragged and wretched looking man, who took his seat upon the bench allotted to prisoners. I imagined from the man's appearance, that his offense was that of yielding to his appetite for intoxicating drinks, and a few moments I found that my suspicions were correct, for the clerk read the complaint, in which the man was charged with being a common drunkard. The case was clearly made out, but before sentence had been passed, I conversed with him for a few moments, and found that he was not yet past all hope for reformation. He told me that if he could be saved from the House of Correction, he never again would taste intoxicating liquors, there was such an earnestness in that tone, and a look of firm resolve, that I determined to aid him, I bailed him, by permission of the Court. He was ordered to appear for sentence in three weeks from that time. He signed the pledge and became a sober man; at the expiration of this period of probation, I accompanied him into the court room. The Judge expressed himself much pleased with the account we gave of the man, and instead of the usual penalty—imprisonment in the House of Correction—he fined him one cent and costs amounting in all to $3.76, which was immediately paid. The man continued industrious and sober, and without doubt has been by his treatment, saved from a drunkard's grave. (pp. 4-5)

At the beginning of the 20th century, the probation movement expanded. Various states passed legislation and by 1920, probation was available in every state for juvenile offenders and for adults in 33 states (Shelden, 1982). [While probation may have originated for humanitarian reasons, its continued growth appears related to monetary concerns.] As Shelden (1982) noted, "one survey found that it cost the state about $3,400 a year to keep one youth in a state training school, but it cost one-tenth of this to keep him on probation" (President's Commission, 1967).

In the case of parole, this approach was also rooted in the English practice. The term comes from the French word *parole d'honneur*, which means "word of honor" (McCarthy & McCarthy, 1984). The early practice of parole in England involved the banishment of criminals to the colonies—including America. Also, it included "tickets of leave"—the practice of offering early release to inmates for a variety of reasons, including good behavior, meritorious service, or marriage. Parole was introduced as law in 1853 and for prisoners sentenced to terms of 15 years or more, they were required to serve six years prior to being considered for release. The United States' practice of parole was spearheaded by Zebulon Brockway, the superintendent of the Elmira Reformatory, in 1876. His efforts resulted in the concept of the indeterminate sentence. When correctional authorities thought the inmate was ready to be released, he was granted his freedom for a six month period of parole under the supervision of a volunteer. By 1900, parole was available in 20 states (McCarthy & McCarthy, 1984).

THE ORGANIZATION OF SERVICES

The basic concepts of probation and parole are similar for both the United States and Japan. Probation means that a convicted adult or juvenile is sentenced by a judge for either a determinate or indeterminate period of time in the community under the direct supervision of a probation officer. Parole means an individual is released into the community prior to the expiration of his or her sentence, but is placed under supervision of an officer until the sentence expires.

In Japan "probation" officers provide both probation and parole services. In the United States, there are often different agencies for each function, and hence both probation officers and parole officers. This is a major difference in the organization of services.

Japan's Approach

In Japan, the Rehabilitation Bureau of the Ministry of Justice is the adminstrative agency charged with providing rehabilitation services for the nation. It is one of seven agencies within the Minis-

Ministry of Justice — Tokyo

Tokyo Probation Office

try of Justice, and it has four divisions: General Affairs, Investigation and Liaison, Supervision and the Amnesty Division. The apparatus includes a National Offenders Rehabilitation Commission attached to the Ministry of Justice. Its functions include:

1. Recommendation of pardons, for individuals who have been initially reviewed by the appropriate officials at probation offices, prisons or public prosecutors' offices.
2. Review of appeals of decisions to deny parole rendered by local or regional offices.

The Commission itself consists of five members who are appointed by the Minister of Justice with the consent of the Japanese Diet (Parliament).

There are eight regional parole boards in Japan that review applications for parole from prisons and training schools. They sit in panels of three. They also have the authority to revoke the parole of individuals based on recommendations of local offices. Organized under the regional offices are the 50 local probation/parole offices in each of the prefectures (four offices are located on Hokkaido Island).

Decentralization of Probation Services

Historically, Japanese probation facilities were not always as decentralized as they are today. Typically, major offices existed in the large cities like Tokyo, Yokohama, and Kyoto and probation workers had to oversee their volunteers and clients out of these large municipal offices. Now, in addition to the 50 main offices, there are 25 branch offices throughout Japan. Also, since 1980 greater use has been made of "day offices" or local facilities in which weekly or monthly meetings are arranged. Typically "day offices" are rooms in municipal buildings, public halls, or youth centers and activities reflect the work of the large offices—interviewing of probationers, supervision of volunteers, family counseling, consultation with school teachers and employers and liaison with community agencies (my field study led me to a visit to a day office in the Yokohama area).

As noted above, the term "probation officer" in Japan refers to the person who provides parole services as well as probation services. Subsequent references to Japan's probation officers will primarily refer to their work in the parole field, as the focus of this work is on services for offenders released from incarceration.

Japan's service is essentially a national one although, as noted above, services are decentralized through the 50 local probation/parole offices in each of the prefectures. Just 792 officers existed in all of Japan in 1983. Unlike some of their American counterparts, they don't carry firearms! For example, parole officers in New York state carry a pistol.

In Japan there is only one "association" for all personnel. It's purpose is to negotiate salaries and it serves a social function, but it has no power to strike. In contrast, in the United States many correctional employees, not just probation and parole personnel, are members of unions. By 1970, one-third of all public employees in America were members of unions. One of the fastest growing unions in the country was the American Federation of State, County, and Municipal Employees (National Advisory Commission on Criminal Justice Standards and Goals, 1976). These unions not only concerned themselves with traditional matters of wages, benefits, and working conditions, but they reached into matters of policy, goals, and staffing. Thus, unions have been a far more powerful force in community based corrections in America than have been the much weaker "associations" in Japan.

Prisoners are eligible for consideration for parole if they have served one third of a fixed term of imprisonment or ten years of a life sentence and "show genuine reformation." Concerning young offenders, one third of the prescribed minimum term of an indeterminate sentence imposed on a juvenile under 20 years of age must be served before parole, and a person sentenced to life imprisonment while under 20 years of age may be released on parole after serving seven years.

The regional parole board will consider an individual for release upon the request of the warden or director of the institution where the inmate is confined. The board then will inquire into the individual's character, behavior at the institution, conduct prior to commitment and other related circumstances. The board places a great deal of emphasis upon the environmental setting to which the individual will return and his or her prospects for rehabilitation. An appraisal of the community's attitude toward a prospective release will also be included. One member of the board always conducts a personal interview with the candidate. Also, the board at its own discretion may conduct hearings on a prisoner's application after receiving a recommendation on the matter from the warden or director of the institution where the individual is incarcerated.

Parole release conditions are determined partly by law and partly through administrative action. For example, parolees must (a) maintain a fixed residence and pursue a lawful occuption; (b) refrain from associating with persons having criminal or delinquent tendencies; (c) maintain good behavior; (d) obtain advance permission from a parole supervisor before changing a place of residence or travelling for an extended period; and (e) comply with any special conditions imposed by the parole board at the time of release. Conditions of probationary supervision are essentially the same in Japan.

In principle, a paroled individual remains under supervision for the unexpired portion of the original sentence of imprisonment. A life-termer released on parole is placed under supervision for life.

Of course, parole may be revoked if a parolee is again convicted of an offense or if he violates a condition of parole. If a violation of parole occurs, or a new criminal act is engaged in by the parolee, then a decision to revoke will be made by the regional parole board within the jurisdiction where the person is being supervised. Of course, minor violations of parole which come to the attention of the supervising officer may be resolved between the officer and his supervisee, or in some cases the matter may be referred by the officer to his supervisor in the local office.

After revocation, the offender serves the unexpired portion of his sentence and, of course, he may be required to serve additional time for a new offense. He may be released on parole again at a later time.

Over half of all Japanese offenders have been paroled since 1945 with the rate climbing to 67 percent at one point, but it decreased to a rate of 51.1 percent in 1978. While parole rates varied in the United States from 100 percent in New Hampshire to 7 percent in Wyoming in 1970, the average nationwide was 64 percent in 1976 (Carter & Wilkins, 1976). In Japan, the lengthier the prison term, the higher the proportion of prisoners paroled—the rate is 75 percent for persons sentenced to terms of five years or more.

Also, it should be noted that half of all parolees experience parole supervision for not more than two months and two thirds of parolees do not exceed three months. Japanese probation officers commented during interviews that the relatively short periods in which ex-offenders were under their supervision made it difficult for them to make an impact on the lives of their supervisees.

Data presented by the Ministry of Justice (National Statement of Japan, 1980) revealed that in 1978 more than 90 percent of all parolees completed their parole terms without revocation. The report goes on to note that recidivism rates for those released between 1971 and 1975 ranged from 19.9 percent to 23.6 percent based on subsequent convictions and sentences to imprisonment within three years. This contrasted with a rate varying from 41.2 percent to 47.5 percent among those directly released after completing their full sentences in prison. Comparable figures for the United States show that in a three year follow-up study of parolees released from state institutions in 1970, 30.3 percent were either reconvicted of offenses or returned to prison as parole violators (Shelden, 1982).

In Japan inmates have no right to submit an application for parole. When the warden of a prison finds that an inmate is ready for parole, he submits an application for release to the appropriate regional parole board. As one retired Japanese probation officer complained, "Parole boards have the authority to take the initiative in such matters but they do not. Therefore, there are shorter periods of parole (and perhaps fewer parolees) due to this conservative policy practiced by correctional institutions' officials."

Article 28 of the Japanese Penal Code stipulates that "when a person sentenced to imprisonment with or without forced labor demonstrates genuine reformation he may be paroled by an action of administrative authorities after he has served one-third of the sentence of a limited term, or ten years of a life sentence" (Suzuki, 1982). The Penal Code goes on to note that the candidate for parole be repentant, desire rehabilitation, be unlikely to recidivate and be a person society will accept on parole. Repentance is a critical factor in Japan. It is one that frequently came up in conversations with Japanese officials. As in the United States, where somewhat similar parole conditions apply, it is one thing to stipulate these criteria in law, but quite another to apply them effectively in screening applicants.

Parole Boards in Japan

As already noted, in Japan one board member interviews the applicant, while three others evaluate the individual's overall record. The author interviewed the Section Chief of the Kanto Regional Parole Board, a Mr. Tomita. The Kanto board is one of eight in Japan and includes the densely populated Tokyo area. Tomita-san had earlier worked in his career as a public prosecutor before being appointed to the Kanto Board. Interestingly, other public prosecutors have also found their way on to parole boards throughout Japan. While senior probation officers late in their careers are increasingly appointed to these prestigious posts, historically public prosecutors more often occupied these tribunals. Occasionally, one finds a prison administrator on a board. One of the advantages of such an appointment is that one can retire after 60. It's the author's impression that many policy making positions at Japan's Ministry of Jus tice (which embraces Corrections, Probation and Public Prosecutional functions) are dominated by individuals who originally started their careers as public prosecutors. The Kanto Board processes roughly one-third of all the applications for parole in the country. Nationwide data for 1981 revealed that 50.9 percent of all adults discharged from prison were released on parole.

During the interview, the author inquired about the application of the death penalty to which Tomita replied "it depends upon the particular Minister of Justice and his relationship with colleagues in the Diet." The law allowed the Minister of Justice to exercise some discretion in ordering or restricting executions. The parole chief added, "even a lifer is eligible for parole after ten years." Data for 1981 on "life termers," as the Japanese call them, are presented in Table 1.

TABLE 1

Years Served By Those Sentenced to Life,
Prior to Release on Parole - 1981

Source: Kanto Regional Parole Board, 1983

Total	under 13 ys	-14	-15	-16	-17	-18	-19	-20	20 yrs or more
57	2	6	17	13	6	8	2	2	1

Haberman (1984) stated that while 570 Japanese have been executed since World War II, the death sentence was administered only 12 times in 1976, once in 1980 and not at all since then. Capital punishment can be imposed for 17 different offenses, but has most commonly been reserved for those who have committed murder or for killing someone during a robbery. While recent data are not available, in 1980 only 14 percent of the respondents to a government survey favored abolition of the death penalty.

Critics of American courts have pointed to the disparity in sentences as justifying the need for reform and Tomita readily acknowledged that disparity in sentencing was characteristic of the Japanese judiciary. He commented, "Crimes that may result in a life sentence may be the judgement of one judge, but another given the same conditions might give just 15 years." He reiterated some points heard earlier:

Demonstrating repentance and progress while in prison (good behavior) are critical factors in obtaining early release. Of course, the person's likelihood of recidivating is taken into account along with his or her prospects for readjusting in the community upon release. It is in this context that the probation officer's report (including those of the volunteer probation officer) will be considered. If the family is unwilling to take the individual back, a common occurrence among chronic offenders, then the person will probably be sent to a rehabilitation aid hostel (halfway house). About 25 percent of all released adult offenders go to halfway houses. This is particularly true of older offenders—perhaps those over age 40. Also, another factor in considering placement in a hostel is that the parents of older offenders may have died or the family may have resided in a rural area, while the ex-offender had lived in an urban setting and may be uncomfortable in returning to an agrarian setting. In the case of juveniles, the peer group may be the major problem. Historically, an uncle or aunt might have been willing to look after a released juvenile, but today family relationships aren't as strong and therefore it's more difficult to place a juvenile with a relative. For this reason we occasionally release a juvenile to a halfway house, but there is currently just one facility in the Tokyo area. As youngsters get older some move away from criminal activity. Among *bosozoku* (young gangs of motorcycle riders) there is a transiency that we have observed. Group leaders change from year to year. Interviews we've had conducted with leaders who have been sent to training schools indicated that other leaders have filled the void while they were incarcerated and they express less desire to rejoin their gangs upon release. Most assaults by *bosozoku* members are against other gang members or even among their own ranks not against the public.

Applications for parole come to the board from prisons, juvenile training schools and womens' guidance homes. In Japan in 1981, 15,028 adults were released on parole while 14,474 were released directly.

While in theory the main purpose of parole is to aid the rehabilitation of the offender, one probation official accused prison administrators of unloading disruptive inmates who threatened prison security onto the parole system. He went on to claim that too often parole boards acquiesed to correctional authorities in these matters.

The United States' Approach

Unlike in Japan, where probation and parole continue to be accepted as componenets of the justice system, they are under attack in the United States. The General Accounting Office issued a report in 1982 that stated that the parole system was "riddled with inconsistency, contradiction, and inefficiency" (United Press International, 1982). Parole, more than probation, has been attacked. Parole boards, and the system of supervision they have offered have been banished in many states. In 1985, the U.S. Congress approved legislation phasing out parole in the federal system over a five year period. Nonetheless, as of 1979 more than two-thirds of all adult offenders released were placed on parole (National Council on Crime and Delinquency, 1979).

There are federal, state, and county probation and parole systems, but there is no one policy making body comparable to Japan's Rehabilitation Bureau that is charged with overseeing all activities in this field.

Overall, on any given day, there were approximately 550,000 adult offenders under some form of supervision in the United States in 1977 (Shelden, 1982). This estimate includes approximately 10,000 under supervision in community homes, and another 540,000 either on probation or parole. For juveniles, there were 178,000 on probation or parole and another 9,700 in community homes during 1977.

The American Correctional Association has identified four different organizational structures used to administer parole in the

United States. In the majority of states, parole boards administer both the probation and parole system. A second approach involves separate probation and parole agencies, while in a third approach parole and prison services are unified. Finally, a fourth approach combines probation, parole and prison services under one agency umbrella. As McCarthy & McCarthy (1984) noted:

> The ideal structure for parole services administration is a subject of debate. Service continuity and coordination is enhanced by combining services under one organizational umbrella. But separating probation and parole from institutional corrections may permit these services to be more responsive to the orders of the courts and parole board respectively. (p. 249)

The myriad of agencies includes approximately 3,868 state and local governmental agencies with responsibility for probation, parole, or some combination of the two (Smykla, 1984). This excludes federal operations. Contrast those numbers with the eight regional and 50 prefectural offices within the Japanese system.

Parole Boards in the United States

While many public prosecutors and senior probation/parole officials make up the ranks of parole board members in Japan, the situation is very different in the United States.

O'Leary and Hanrahan (1977) reported in detail on who becomes appointed to parole boards. Many states require no knowledge of corrections or law to qualify for membership. For that matter, there are no legally stipulated requirements of any kind in Arkansas, Georgia, Hawaii, Louisiana, Nevada, New Hampshire, New Mexico, New York, and Oklahoma to name just several. A few states stipulate requirements for the parole board chairman such as "knowledge of parole, rehabilitation, and kindred subjects," but do not specify requirements for members. In Delaware, the chairman must have a graduate degree in social work, sociology, psychology, criminology or corrections and five years experience in corrections (O'Leary and Hanrahan, 1977). Often though, when requirements exist for members, they are vague such as in Florida where the law states, "knowledge of penology and social welfare." Typically, state governors make the appointments.

Parole boards have almost total discretionary power to determine which inmates are to be released on parole. Parole is considered a privilege, not a right, and the United States Supreme Court has observed that "nothing in the Constitution requires a State to provide for probation or parole" (Reid, 1985, p. 602). Therefore, in both Japan and the United States the government initiates the release process. Inmates in both countries have no "right" to parole and decision-making power is vested in correctional authorities and parole boards, where they still exist.

Costs are always a consideration, for the public as well as justice officials, in deciding on alternatives of probation, incarceration, parole, and community-based treatment. In 1983, the average annual cost for one federal parolee or probationer was $1,300 while a non-federal parolee or probationer cost between $220 and $1,700. Maintaining a prisoner in a federal facility cost an average of $13,000 per year while incarcerating an offender in a state facility ranged between $5,000 and $23,000. The average annual cost for an adult offender at a state halfway house was $12,000 while at a local community based facility the cost was $8,000 (Bureau of Justice Statistics, 1983).

Parole board members must work within legal and administrative guidelines and policies. As Reid (1985) has observed, their decisions have a serious and lasting impact on inmates' lives, and they operate in the "spotlight of public opinion" when well-known offenders are considered for parole (p. 602). Predictions of success, using both *clinical* and *statistical* models, have yielded mixed results and this has provided ammunition for those who have sought to eliminate parole and replace it with a determinate sentencing type of structure. Even with flat term laws, inmates are able to earn an early release based on the accumulation of "good time." Parole boards have used criteria such as age, education, and past criminal history, along with behavior within the institution, in deciding who is suitable for parole. Balancing the prospects of an inmate successfully re-integrating into the community versus the risk to the community has proved to be a difficult assignment for parole boards. Critics have charged that racial and socio-economic factors have been allowed to bias the judgment of parole boards resulting in arbitrary and capricious decisions as to who is released.

Once released, parolees must abide by conditions that mirror those in Japan. In actual fact, since Japan has borrowed so much from the United States in the field of probation and parole, one suspects that they have modeled their conditions after those in the

United States. Here are some of the conditions required in California (Shelden, 1982):

1. You must have permission from your parole agent to change residence or leave the county of your residence.
2. It is necessary to maintain gainful employment. Any change in employment must be reported to and approved by the parole agent.
3. You must submit a monthly report to your agent, unless otherwise directed by your parole agent.
4. You must refrain from using alcoholic beverages to an excess.
5. You may not possess, use or traffic in any narcotic drug.
6. You shall not own, possess, use, sell, nor have under your control any weapons or firearms.
7. You must avoid association with former inmates unless approved by your parole agent and you must not associate with persons of bad reputation.
8. Before operating a motor vehicle you must have permission from your parole agent and you must have a valid driver's license.
9. You must cooperate at all times with your parole agent.
10. You must obey all laws and conduct yourself as a good citizen.

(p. 408)

As mentioned earlier, in Japan one member of the parole board interviews the application. Once again, in the United States, with its many jurisdictions, procedures vary tremendously. In some cases the entire board interviews the candidate, while in other instances only part of the board interviews. A few jurisdictions use hearing examiners to interview inmates, and in some states no interviews are conducted—decisions are based soley on written reports.

Parole Revocation in Japan and the United States

In Japan parole revocation is made by the regional parole board which has jurisdiction over the locality of the probation/parole office in charge of the supervision of a person on parole. The ruling of revocation is in response to the request of the chief of the local office. The following are general conditions of parole and when violated can result in revocation:

1. The requirement to live at a specified residence and to engage in lawful occupation;
2. The restriction of bad conduct;

3. The restriction of associating with criminal types;
4. The requirement to seek previous approval for move of residence or long journey.

In addition to the general conditions, the parolee is also required to abide by special conditions which the parole board sets forth as a guide. Special conditions vary widely as they are designed to meet the individual need of each parolee. Those in frequent use include restriction of alcoholic beverages, regular contact with the volunteer probation officer and support of the family, to mention a few. Failure to comply with a special condition can be a cause of reincarceration exactly in the same way as a violation of a general condition may result in revocation of parole.

In the United States, while procedures vary from state to state, parole revocation must provide certain "due process" to the parolee. *Generally, the entire system of justice in the United States—at all stages of arrest, trial, incarceration and release—offers a greater consideration for the rights of the individual.* For example, as McCarthy & McCarthy (1984) point out, there is a two stage hearing procedure that the United States Supreme Court has ruled on.

> At the first stage, a preliminary hearing is held before an uninvolved person or impartial officer—not necessarily a judicial official—who determines if there is reasonable cause to believe that parole conditions were violated. The offender is provided notice of the hearing and a full description of the charges At the second stage, the formal revocation proceeding takes place before the parole board or its representative. Minimum due process protection provided to the offender at this stage includes:
>
> 1. Written notice of the charge
> 2. Disclosure of evidence against him
> 3. The right to be heard in person and present witnesses and evidence in his own behalf
> 4. A right to confront and cross-examine adverse witnesses (unless good cause is found not permitting the interaction)
> 5. A neutral and detached hearing body (such as a parole board)
> 6. A written statement by the fact finders explaining the decision

(p. 256)

As in Japan, the actual conditions of parole are the basis for revoking parole. There are two types of parole violations, legal and technical. A legal violation takes place if a new crime is committed by a parole while a technical violation occurs if the person violates one of the conditions of parole. Revocation of technical grounds is not automatic and depends on the discretion exercised by the parole officer. Some technical violations may be ignored by the officer. Conditions vary from state to state.

As noted at the outset of this work, probation and parole are under fire in the United States and many parole boards have been banded. In Japan, perhaps because of low crime rates and few violent offenders, that part of their system is not "under the gun" and is not being scrutinzed by reform minded criminologists and politicians. In this context, the author wishes to conclude this chapter by mentioning some of the recent press controversy surrounding parole in the United States. Two homicides committed by parolees during early 1984 helped to fuel the discussion.

In one case, a police officer was killed by a 24 year old parolee with a long arrest record. During the subsequent controversy which raged in the press, New York City's Fortune Society, a group of former inmates dedicated to assisting ex-offenders, presented a different viewpoint. Members argued that as long as nothing was being done for the offender while he was in prison then it was hard to expect released offenders to be law abiding upon their return to society. Staff of the Fortune Society noted that trades that inmates are taught have little application outside prison and that they are not counseled about what life will be like when they get out. Romeo Sanchez, 33, who had been on parole twice and had become a drug addict at 17, stated he was taught sewing. He commented, "when you're released from prison you're out of touch, and when you hit New York you're scared" (Greer, 1984).

Generally, the ex-offender members of the Fortune Society were not in favor of abolishing the system. As David Rothenberg, the Executive Director and Founder of the Fortune Society said, "Parole should not be eliminated; right now parole is a starting point" (Greer, 1984, p. 27). He further commented that education was one of the major needs. Of the 2,000 former convicts who participated in their program every year, on the average they had a third grade education.

New York parole officer Robert Denison (1984) in an angry letter to *The New York Times*, commented on the discussion in his state concerning the abolishment of the parole system.

> Regardless of whether the Board of Parole is abolished, community supervision is essential for the following reasons:
>
> New York State parole officers are currently supervising more than 28,000 parolees. The vast majority of these parolees have committed violent crimes and/or have lengthy arrest records. Nevertheless, only a very small percentage (less than 3 percent annually) are convicted of new crimes while under parole supervision, and many of their crimes are nonviolent.
>
> If a detailed statistical study were undertaken, I'm sure one would find that during the time the typical parolee is under supervision he has far fewer arrests than in any other period in his criminal history (and in the majority of cases none).
>
> It should also be noted that the parole officer, who assists the parolee with employment, drug, alcohol and mental-hygiene counseling, is almost always the first person contacted by the parolee's family in any emergency regarding the parolee.
>
> Parole officers also greatly contribute to society's desire to improve "law and order" by revoking the parole of those who violate parole rules and regualtions before they have an opportunity to commit new crimes. (Parole officers are peace officers who make their own arrests.)
>
> Furthermore, most district attorneys are extremely thankful that there is a parole officer to send a parolee back to prison. In all instances of new arrests, the parole officer conducts an independent investigation, and while lack of evidence "beyond a reasonable doubt" may make it impossible to convict a parolee in a court of law, his parole can be revoked on the strength of a "preponderance of evidence." In these instances, a parole officer even acts as an attorney in presenting the state's case.
>
> It's tragic when a parolee commits a violent crime against anyone, be it a police officer or a civilian (even if this occurs in only a small percentage of cases), but please don't listen to those who advocate the elimination of supervision, because then society will truly suffer.

Some have argued convincingly, like Wallace Cheatham, that the whole idea of claiming that "rehabilitation had proven to be a failure" was totally inaccurate as applied to probation and parole because services have been grossly underfunded and neglected (Cheatham, 1984).

REFERENCES

Bureau of Justice Statistics. *Report to the Nation on Crime and Justice: The Data*, Washington, D.C.: United States Government Printing Office, 1983.

Carter, R. and Wilkins, L. *Probation, Parole and Community Corrections*, New York: John Wiley & Sons, Inc., 1976.

Cheatham, W. "On Faulting Nonexistent Rehabilitation." *The New York Times*, Monday, May 14, 1984 p. A14.

Denison, R. "The Worth of a Parole Officer's Work." Letter to *The New York Times*, Friday, March 9, 1984, p. A28.

Greer, W. "Ex-Convicts Fault Justice System; Contend It Fails Inmates." *The New York Times*, Saturday, February 25, 1984, p. 27.

Haberman, C. "Japanese Gallows: Case of the 'Wrong Man'," *The New York Times*, July 22, 1984, p. 8.

Lindner, C. and Savarese, M. "The Evolution of Probation." *Federal Probation*, March, 1984, Volume 48, No. 1, pp. 3–10.

McCarthy, B. R. and B. J. McCarthy. *Community-Based Corrections*. Monterey, California: Brooks/Cole Publishing Company, 1984.

National Advisory Commission on Criminal Justice Standards and Goals, "Organization and Administration of Corrections," in R. M. Carter and L. T. Wilkins *Probation, Parole and Community Corrections*. New York: John Wiley & Sons, Inc., 1976.

National Council on Crime and Delinquency, *Parole in the United States: 1979*, Washington, D.C.: U.S. Department of Justice, 1979.

National Statement of Japan. "Crime Prevention and the Quality of Life," Japanese Ministry of Justice, 1980.

New York Probation Association. "John Augustus First Probation Officer," 1939, pp. 3–4. From "A Report of the Labors of John Augustus, For the Last Ten Years, in Aid of the Unfortunate," Boston: Wright & Hasty, 1852.

O'Leary, V. and Hanrahan, K. *Parole Systems in the United States: A Detailed Description of Their Structure and Procedures*, 3rd ed., Hackensack, New Jersey: National Council on Crime and Delinquency, 1977.

Parker, L. C. Japan's Volunteer Probation Officer System Offers Cheap But Viable Approach to Reform, *The Japan Times*, August 23, 1983, Op-Ed page.

Rehabilitation Bureau. "Community-Based Treatment of Offenders in Japan," Ministry of Justice, 1981.

Reid, S. T. *Crime and Criminology*, New York: Holt, Rinehart & Winston, 1985.

Shelden, R. *Criminal Justice in America: A Sociological Approach*. Boston & Toronto: Little, Brown and Company, 1982.

Smykla, J. *Probation and Parole: Crime Control in the Community*. New York: Macmillan Publishing Company, 1984.

Susuki, K. "Halfway Houses in Japan," unpublished manuscript, United Nations Asia Far East Institute for the Prevention of Crime and Treatment of Offenders, 1978 (amended for the author, 1983).

Suzuki, Tetsuo. "The Existing Parole System in Japan," unpublished paper, Japanese Ministry of Justice, 1982.

Tanigawa, A. chapter 18, "Public Participation and the Integrated Approach in Japanese Rehabilitation Services," in *Criminal Justice Asia: The Quest For An Integrated Approach*, United Nations Asia Far East Institute for the Prevention of Crime and Treatment of Offenders, 1982.

Tokyo Probation Office. "Profile of the Tokyo Probation Office," unpublished mimeographed statement, 1983.

United Press International. "Probationers Found to Outnumber Prisoners," *The New York Times*, Wednesday, August 18, 1982, p. A10.

CHAPTER V

The Role of the Professional Worker

THE PAROLE OFFICER in both the United States and Japan suffers from role conflict—he is both friend and foe. On the one hand, the officer is expected to be a counselor with the parolee, yet having to endure massive caseloads, he has little time to render personal assistance. In contrast, the officer is expected to conduct surveillance on the released offender's activities and he or she must be prepared to "violate" the parolee if he veers too far from the conditions of parole. One need only observe the sidearm carried by some American parole officers to be reminded of the stress on the law enforcement function in the United States. Japanese parole officers do not carry weapons. Rarely, are they called upon to supervise dangerous offenders. If a dangerous situation is anticipated, the police are called.

In this chapter the author will offer a few words about the role of the American officer before embarking on a more in depth look at the role and function of the Japanese worker. Various field offices around Japan provided the setting for this portrait.

In general, while the parole board and top administration do much to shape the policy, and consequently the behavior of the line officer there is still ample opportunity for the officer to interpret his or her own role. Given this freedom of action, the personality of the worker comes into play. Officers may emphasize the law enforcement dimension by spending a major share of their time "acting as vigilantes and going out of their way to watch their parolees committing infractions" (Shelden, 1982, p. 409), or officers may spend a disproportionate share of time counseling and relating to a handful of offenders while neglecting the 100 odd others on the caseload.

In addition to the conflict posed between being a counselor and enforcing the law, parole officers lack community resources and are often inadequately trained for their jobs (Bartolas, 1981). On the other hand, parole officers in the United States are usually better paid than probation officers and therefore tend to be older and more experienced in the criminal justice system.

It's the researcher's impression that American officers, as in police work, experience greater job stress than do their colleagues in Japan. This is accounted for, in part, by the larger caseload that must be handled directly unlike in Japan where the huge cadre of volunteers act as intermediaries. In a study of the workload of federal officers it was found that 28.7 percent of the typical officer's time was spent supervising clients. This averaged out to just 6.4 hours per year per client (Shelden, 1982).

Furthermore, the United States officer has more violent and dangerous offenders to contend with on his or her caseload. This is bound to tax the most competent professional. The current expression is "burnout." It is generally defined to mean a state of emotional exhaustion and cynicism.

Any number of studies of stress among American police officers have pointed to the fact that tension between administrators and line officers is a major source of stress within police organizations. This problem appears to be equally true for those working with ex-offenders. Shelden's (1982) statement of the demands of the administrative hierarchy on the parole officer speaks to this point:

> The parole officer, it must be remembered, works within the parole system and is under constant pressure to be "on top" of a case. That is, the parole officer must be constantly aware of what each parolee is doing. If there is a "blow up," that is, if the parolee commits a new crime, the parole officer must be prepared to answer to those above. In order to do this, he or she must maintain a readiness to *strictly* enforce the rules. The parole officer has a strong desire to please the parole board, and in many cases the parole board is reluctant to return a parolee to prison on one minor technical violation (although this does happen). Irwin found that parole officers tend to "bank" incidents of violations of parole rules. The parole officer is preparing for the possibility of having to build a strong case. He or she may make a mental note or record in the log of every minor violation committed by the parolee. (p. 410)

In addition, Smykla (1984) has noted that burnout is a major problem among both United States probation and parole officers and cited studies to document his view. Previously dedicated workers become disillusioned and callous with their clients or leave the field. Whitehead (1982) in a study of 700 probation officers found widespread burnout. Those surveyed expressed more intense feelings of being overextended and exhausted by their work than did samples of workers in other human services fields such as nursing, education, and social work. Probation officers also claimed they were less personally involved and felt a lower sense of achievement than did workers in the other fields. Twenty-five percent of the probation workers were dissatisfied with their careers in probation and another 21 percent were undecided. More than half felt underpaid and 90 percent said there were no promotional opportunities in their agencies.

The job required the officer to assist released offenders in coping with problems of reintegrating into the community. This includes assistance in obtaining housing and a job along with helping the ex-inmate reunite with family and friends if he has any available. However, with limited time available for an individual case, given the large caseload size, the parolee is often forced to fend for himself.

The most common forms of supervision require the parolee to periodically come in for an office visit. Occasionally, an officer will make an unannounced visit to the individual's home, particularly if there is reason to believe the person has dishonestly stated some facts about his living situation.

Experimental Programs in the United States

Any number of administrators and policy makers in the probation and parole field, while acknowledging the shortcomings of large officer-offender ratios, have sought to experiment with caseload size as a means of improving service and reducing recidivism rates. Recently, New Jersey and Georgia have experimented with probationers.

The program in Georgia looks particularly promising. In this experimental program, 575 felons have worked under intensive supervision with a team of two probation officers who carry caseloads of just 25 (*New York Times*, 1984). A standard caseload in Georgia is 75, with once a month contacts. Judges have the final word on candidates selected for the program, but usually candidates are non-violent offenders who have already been convicted and sentenced to prison. Probationers stay on the program for at least six months. They must meet a mandatory 8 p.m. curfew, work at least 136 hours in public service jobs and have at least *five* contacts a week with the assigned probation officer. Intensive probation costs $1,200 per year compared to the usual cost of $300 per year, but the low rate of recidivism—fewer than 5 percent of the participants committed crimes while in the program—is very impressive. Imprisoning an offender in Georgia currently costs more than $10,000 per year so, of course, this is also a factor in whether the state will consider adopting the program on a more permanent basis.

Contract parole or Mutual Agreement Programming (MAP) has been tried in a number of states (Bartollas, 1981). Under MAP, parole boards, correctional departments and inmates agree to a three-way contractual arrangement. Prisoners take the lead in planning individually tailored rehabilitative programs to obtain parole at a mutually agreed upon future date. The approach includes a statement of what the inmate is supposed to do to earn release. Rules are developed and put into writing and signed by all parties. A schedule is established that gives the inmate time to achieve his or her goals and allows the staff to evaluate progress toward the agreed upon criteria. A number of states adopted it in the 1970's and most — including Maryland, Florida, Maine, Georgia, Massachuetts, and Wisconsin have continued with it. However, any number of criticisms of the approach have surfaced. For example, some parole boards have viewed MAP as usurping its decision-making authority and correctional authorities have sometimes failed to deliver the key resources or programs in the contractual arrangement. Finally, evaluations of MAP in Wisconsin and Michigan revealed that it was not superior to traditional forms of parole release (McCarthy & McCarthy, 1984).

The Japanese Officer

The role of the Japanese probation/parole officer is quite different from that of his American counterpart principally because of the key role played by the volunteer. Because large numbers of volunteers directly serve the ex-inmates clients of the system, the professional's role is primarily administrative. The Japanese officer is a coordinator, consultant, and most importantly a supervisor of the volunteer worker who handles most of the face to face contact with parolees. The professional is required to intervene directly when the volunteer runs into difficulty with clients, when the parolee's family asks for help or when police involvement comes in to play (Sasaki, 1983).

A reminder to the reader, Japan's probation officer performs both probation and parole activities as noted earlier. Listed below is a statement of the functions performed by Japanese probation officers (Tokyo Probation Office, 1983):

1. Supervision of probationers and parolees at all age levels.
2. Assist in the adjustment of family members and other social conditions for inmates awaiting release from correctional institutions.
3. Provision of aftercare for offenders discharged from penal, correctional and detaining institutions who lack supervision.
4. Investigation of applicants for pardons.
5. Interpretation of rehabilitative concepts to the public; the improvement of the social environment and promotion of activities of local citizens with a view to the prevention of crime.
6. Recommendation and selection of volunteer probation officers.
7. Supervision of rehabilitation aid societies (halfway houses).

Japan's integrated or quasi-national system of probation and parole allows one to generalize a lot more about their service than is the case in the United States with its fragmented system of county, state, and federal services. Thus, although each of the 47 prefectural governments in Japan provides some of the financial support and retains a nominal influence over the probation and parole services it is fundamentally a national system.

Observing activities, interviewing officials, and sitting in on sessions between probation officers (both volunteers and professionals) and their clients in offices in Tokyo, Yokohama, Kofu, Chiba and Kyoto formed the core of the field research and it offered a representative picture of Japan's approach in this field. Not surprisingly, given its national character, operations in Chiba were quite similar to those in Kyoto, etc. The Tokyo operation, however is a bit different.

PROFILE OF THE TOKYO PROBATION OFFICE

Perhaps because Tokyo is the largest city, and of course the capital, probation and parole activities have a distinctive flavor. Experimental programs are more apt to be launched here, perhaps because the Ministry of Justice is nearby. For the same reason, the atmosphere in the office seemed a bit more formal.

In 1981, the Tokyo office budget was 830 million yen ($3.7 million), including expenses for volunteers and subsidies offered to halfway houses in that jurisdiction. Probation officers (including administrators) increased from 57 to 59 from 1981 to 1983. The office included 15 women. The breakdown in staff for 1983 was as follows:

Director	1
Deputy Director	1
Chiefs of Sections	5
Chief of Hachioji Branch	1
Senior Probation Officers	12
Probation Officers	47
Secretaries and Clerks	22
Others	4
Total	93

The above figures excludes the volunteer probation officers. The organizational chart for the Tokyo office is presented below:

	-General Affairs Section	-General Affairs Unit
		-Accounting Unit
		-Planning & Liaison Unit
	-Investigation & Liaison Section	-V.P.O. Training Unit
		-Coordination Unit
		-Reception Unit
		-Filing Unit
Director—Deputy Director		-Statistics Unit
	-1st Supervision Section (Largest Section)	Pardons Unit -*Direct Supervision Unit (4 Staff Experimental Unit)

	-Supervision Units
-2nd Supervision Section	-Traffic Cases Unit
	-Supervision Units (23 Districts in Tokyo)
-After-Care Section	-Material Aids Unit
	-Hostel Units (Half-way Houses)
	-Women's Counselling Unit
	-Investigation & Liaison Unit
-Hachioji Branch Office	-Supervision Units
	-Hostel Unit (Half-way Houses)

*The Direct Supervision Unit is experimental. In this unit, professional probation workers engage in direct supervision of clients handling difficult cases such as drug abusers.

Learning about the workings of the Tokyo office was greatly aided by interviews with probation officials Kitazawa, Nishikawa, and Takaike. In an interview with Kitazawa, he noted that as the supervisor of the "1st Supervision Section" his area included *Ohta-ku*, a particularly densely populated area with more than one million people and "more than its share of criminals." Several probation officers worked under him and, in turn, supervised the work of 300 volunteers. He lamented the fact that most volunteers were older (average 60.7 years), echoing the concern of many Japanese officials. In Kitazawa's view, the main activity of the professional is to "control the match-ups between volunteers and ex-offenders; the professionals don't have time for treatment." While acknowledging that the older age of volunteers might represent a handicap for some in their work with young ex-offenders he was quick to point out one of their strengths—"they have a powerful influence in their respective communities, they're often well established." He added, "we like to identify people who have influence to begin with because they can often mobilize resources for their clients." Here is the officially stated procedure for handling cases in the Tokyo office:

    i) Appearance of the client at the office.

    ii) Interview by the probation officer in charge of the case.* Juveniles are handled somewhat differently:

*Tokyo is divided into 32 probation areas. Each area has one or more probation officers. A parolee who is placed at a rehabilitation aid hostel (halfway house) is supervised by the probation officer supervising that hostel.

        a)   juvenile probationers who have committed traffic law offenses and have been placed on the short-term treatment program.

        b)   juvenile and adult probationers under 23 years of age are subject to the Probation Officer's "direct supervision," (e.g. special cases such as drug abusers.)

    iii. Conditions presented as part of written agreement.

        a)   Provision of special conditions for juvenile probationers;

        b)   Report of residence by adult probationers.

    iv) Initial inquiry and summary recording.

    v) Assignment of a volunteer to the case.

    vi) Monthly progress report by the volunteer in charge of the case.

    vii) Supplementary ad hoc reports by the volunteer.

Table 1 offers a sketch of the caseload activity within the Tokyo office at the end of 1982.

The interview with Toshiko Takaike, a woman probation officer in the Tokyo office, proved very illuminating. A bright, energetic woman in her 30's, a few years earlier she had studied counseling in a masters degree program at Santa Clara University in California. This background provided her with knowledge of the U.S. system, and her first point was that in the post World War II period, Japan's system had been initially modeled after the one in the United States.

As an undergraduate student in Japan, she had majored in social work and her classroom instructional materials were usually American in their origin. Noting the greater increase in Japanese materials in the last decade she commented, "we have begun to develop our own psychological and criminological theories and now 25 percent of our texts are Japanese." Elaborating, she stated

TABLE 1

Probation and Parole Supervision:
client categories, period of supervision and number of cases

Source: Tokyo Probation Office, January, 1983

Client categories	Period of Supervision	No. of cases handled in 1982	No. of cases under supervision as of Dec. 31, 1982
Juvenile Probationer (sent from family courts)	until age 20 or for 2 yrs whichever longer	(2,614)* 8,287	(1,666)* 5,156
Training School Parolees	normally until age 20; subject to extension	(36)* 1,396	(34)* 833
Prison Parolees	normally for the remainder of sentence	(257)* 3,105	(55) 927
Adult probationer (sent from criminal courts)	definite period fixed by court between 1 and 5 yrs.	(336)* 2,917	(249) 1,943
Parolees from guidance homes (often prostitutes)	for the remainder of the term of guidance	0	0
Total		(3,264)* 15,705	(2,004)* 8,864

*Parentheses indicate the number of traffic violators.

that most of these newer theories of abnormal behavior were developed by professionals working in Japanese psychiatric hospitals. Notwithstanding her background, professional training in counseling and social work was not the norm for probation officers in Japan. Many were interested in counseling theories and read professional materials, but most identified themselves as "government officers." In contrast, she saw herself as a counselor.

Commenting on the Volunteer Probation Officer system, she admitted that the "generation gap" between volunteers and clients was a major problem but stated, "We have an excellent selection system and can often get very good people with natural talent for this work. Furthermore, we are now selecting volunteers who are under 60 years of age." An additional benefit was the fact that occasionally well to do volunteers gave generous donations to the probation office.

The role conflict posed by being a helper and enforcer was a problem particularly for the professional worker. Charged with the responsibility of enforcing the law, they are occasionally required to violate a client who engages in a serious breach of the conditions of parole or probation. This, of course, creates a barrier to building a trusting relationship. Parolees are often suspicious of the motives of the professionals who supervise them. However, a number of officials pointed to the fact that for this reason volunteers were more successful in building trust through an informal relationship. Almost all volunteers immersed themselves in the helping role, with the professionals being left with administrative tasks, including that of violating offenders.

One of a small group of professionals in her office who worked directly with clients, Takaike claimed she enjoyed her work in the "Direct Treatment Unit." Commenting on her counseling with these clients, she observed:

> Most deny they have any problems. I try to confront them with their situation. One problem is that young people don't want to work. Parents sometimes feed into this by financially supporting their youngsters when these kids should be taking more responsibility. In short, they're spoiled, that's the biggest problem! Parents aren't disciplining their children! A mother may ask a child to be obedient, but if the youngster fails to obey, current thinking is against the use of physical discipline. Individuals over age 40 in our society may have received physical disciplining themselves, but they are unable to apply it to their own children. It also ap-

pears to be part of the more democratic philosophy that has emerged in our society. When I was growing up life was simpler. Delaying gratification of needs was common, but now children seek more immediate gratification.

Summaries of two case studies follow. One was a case prepared by Takaike, while the other was presented orally by Kitazawa in an interview with the author. While superficially they resemble an American approach to a case study, and although they are abbreviated, they provide a glimpse into the kinds of contemporary problems facing Japanese probation officers. Takaike's case study is presented in her own words, with a few grammatical changes offered by the author:

A. Takaike Case Study — Tokyo Probation Office (Summary)

I.   *Background information -* Mr. X (29 years old)
                       Term and category: 17 June 1981 through 16th June
                                      1985 (One year imprisonment with
                                      four years suspension of execution
                                      of sentence) Adult probation

Criminal Offense

Abuse of a stimulant drug (phenyl-methyl-amino-propane 0.1 g) on 9th March 1981 (Violation of Stimulant Drug Control Law)

Guardian and family background:

The guardian who is a friend of his father has been helping him for a long time. His parents died when he was 19 years of age. The family presently consists of a younger brother (21 years of age) who is a university student. The younger brother is a handicapped person who lost his right leg in an accident. The brother was taken care of by his aunt while Mr. X was on remand. Presently, the subject and his younger brother live together in their own house.

Life history:

Mr. X was born in 1951. His father was the president of a major taxi-cab company, whose mistress was Mr. X's mother. In 1965 the subject entered a private high school. In 1968 he completed his high-school education and was admitted to a private university. During his first year (1969), his mother passed away. The sudden death of his father followed six months later. At this time, he left the university and became president of a small company under an umbrella firm of his father's taxi-cab company. In 1980, the taxi-cab company went bankrupt and his company was involved in a breach of trust case. He was arrested during an investigation of this criminal case as he had been using stimulant drugs.

Criminal record:

1978	assault	Y50,000 fine
1978	assault	Y60,000 fine
1980	Violation of Traffic Law (driving without license) three months imprisonment with three years suspension of execution of sentence.	

Physical condition:
Good

Stimulant drug use:

In 1976, a friend introduced him to a gangster, who invited him to Hiroshima and offered him an injection of a stimulant drug. This was the first and only time he had used stimulants up to that time. However, in 1980 he faced problems including bankruptcy and problems in his business which led him to abusing stimulants for tension release.

II.   *Probationary Supervision:*

(1) he was remanded for 80 days and was given the sentence mentioned above. After receiving the sentence, he came to Tokyo Probation Office. Since his case involved the abuse of a stimulant drug, he was put under direct supervision of a professional probation officer.

His plans included his desire to have his own business. However, his guardian (a practicing lawyer) suggested that he work under someone and he secured a job at a haberdasher's shop for him. At the time of the first interview, the probation officer felt that the client looked lonely and uneasy.

(2) The probation officer in charge interviewed him at either

the office or at a place near his shop, taking advantage of holidays. The interviews have been conducted continuously since that time.

The shop has two permanent employees and 40 part-time employees, and is very active. The client has stated that he did not mind working hard; however, he said he felt uneasy at his shop since he had been the president of the company. Since the guardian suggested that Mr. X work there for one year, he has pursued this advice, but hopes to establish his own business with his younger brother a year from now. Presently, he has no friends who are using a stimulant drug. The client's current salary is Y160,000, with which he is not satisfied.

(3) His girlfriend is someone he has known since his school days. The parents of this girl have consented to their marriage. He has been engaged to her since 1982. Her father suggested that he work at his company. Mr. X plans to continue at his present job until June. After that, he is planning to work at her father's company. However, he is very busy at the shop due to the shortage of manpower, and has made up his mind to continue his job. He has confessed his crime and probationary status to his fiancée, but he has not revealed his past to her parents.

(4) Since one year had passed with the client in good standing, the probation officer applied for a tentative release from probationary supervision, which was approved on 30th June 1982.

(5) The situation after the tentative release: the probation officer interviewed the client on 25th March 1983 and noted the following:

Mr. X was married in October of 1982 and presently is working at the trading company which is owned by his father-in-law. The birth of a child is expected in August 1984. It appears that the client has not indulged in stimulant abuse and his condition is stable at this time.

B. *Kitazawa Case Study — Tokyo Probation Office (Summary)*
I.   *Background information* — juvenile parolee, Y.
     This juvenile parolee was released from Odawana Training

School after spending one year there. Paroled in 1982 (the year before) at 17 years of age, the case was still current at the time of my field study in August 1983.

Criminal Offense:

About 27 different incidents of theft. Before being sent to the training school he had been placed under probationary supervision. During that period he fled and was tracked down by his volunteer probation officer, with the assistance of the professional worker in charge. While on his own, without funds or recourse to friends or relatives, he committed the 27 thefts mentioned above. His family situation was quite unique—his father was 90 years old and his mother 70 years of age. The parents had three children with Y being the youngest. None of the three were born to the parents, but were adopted.

From the time of his childhood Y committed minor offenses such as running away from home, shoplifting and getting into trouble at "game centers." As a junior high school student he was placed under probationary supervision, but the treatment offered by the volunteer and supervisor did not appear to make a constructive impact.

Kitazawa interrupted the description of the case to note that some volunteers and their probationers or parolees enjoy excellent relationships—the chemistry is good—while others do not. This affects the frequency of contact. Some clients meet with their supervisors more than twice a month, while others meet less frequently. The fixed schedule of visits, the standard so to speak, was twice a month. Not surprisingly, according to Kitazawa, a strong correlation existed between frequency of visits by volunteer probation officers, and effectiveness (i.e. lower recidivism). Y's experience at the training school had been typical of other juveniles. For the first 45 days he had participated in an orientation program. His program following that was primarily academic in nature—some writing and math, but also "living guidance" and vocational training. The life is very disciplined at these institutions.

On the day the client was paroled he met with the volunteer and professional probation officer at the training school.

His mother and brother also attended this get together. During this session the professional officer explained the conditions of parole and sought to assist the psychological readjustment of the youngster by mentioning some of the issues he would have to face, including some of the idiosyncracies of his parents. The probation officer had become aware of the fact that Y was the least loved of the three siblings. Privately, the probation officer acknowledged to the boy that he should try to get along with his parents and start thinking about employment possibilities and avoid playing around. He would not be returning to school. It should be noted that obligatory education in Japan ceases at age 15.

During this first session the volunteer is assigned. Kitazawa noted, in response to my question, that there is no experimentation with the match-ups between clients and volunteers. He added, "occasionally we have complaints from volunteers that there is too much access and that clients expect too much. This may be related to the fact that they are often well known figures in their local communities. On the other side, clients have been known to complain that their volunteers are too strict, but we rarely respond to these complaints because they're frequently manipulations."

Parole supervision for Y, like that for other offenders, is more intensive (twice a month as noted above) during the first few months. The parole termination date is fixed by law. Under the age of 20, though, termination is discretionary and is typically between six months and one year.

In September of 1982, at the time of discharge, he commenced work at a gasoline service station. He met regularly with his volunteer—twice during September and twice during October. In November he was fired for arguing with a customer and he took on a part-time job while he searched for full time employment. The parents made little effort to help him in this regard. Incidentally, the volunteer in this case was a retired police officer, and this seemed to have a negative effect on the worker's willingness to assist Y in seeking employment.

In January, however, the client found a job in a coffee shop. Initially it was not full time and it was at a low "student" or "arbeito" wage—perhaps 550 yen per hour ($2.25 U.S.). Later he was shifted to the permanent payroll and this arrangement worked well until the shop went bankrupt. Y had worked hard and seemed ambitious. In May he started living with a girl he met at the coffee shop. The mother strongly opposed this arrangement and asked the volunteer to separate them, but he managed to get her to acquiesce to the relationship. In June of 1983, he managed to obtain another position as a cook in another restaurant.

In summary, his relationship with his girlfriend appears to have provided him with some emotional support and given purpose to his life. Therefore, at the time of the interview with Kitazawa, the client was doing well during this latter period of his parole.

FIELD VISITS TO KOFU, CHIBA, YOKOHAMA AND KYOTO

Observations and interviews at various locations outside of Tokyo proved extremely interesting and useful in broadening the author's understanding of Japan's approach to released offenders. This part of the study included visits to "day centers," halfway houses, and probation offices in Kofu, Chiba, Yokohama, and Kyoto. Visits to the homes of volunteers are included in the following chapter. The research in outlying prefectures allowed the investigator to confirm or reject various hypotheses that had been generated as a result of the field investigation in Tokyo. In theory, while probation and parole policies are standard nationwide, subtle differences in operations, nonetheless, emerged in these outlying locations. They may have reflected the tone set by a particular administrator, or more likely the style of a particular group of professionals in charge. The group is always more influential than a single person in Japan. Also, these facilities were always smaller in scale, and this often meant that a more informal and relaxed atmosphere prevailed.

Kofu Visit

Kofu is a case in point. The office in this prefectural capital city of approximately 200,000 residents—small by Japanese standards—provided the parole services and programs for ex-offenders for all of Yamanashi prefecture. It is three hours west of

Tokyo by express train. Kofu is tucked into a narrow valley with lovely mountains rising sharply at its outskirts. From eastern to western boundaries, the prefecture stretches out for approximately 200 kilometers and is much less densely populated than Tokyo prefecture.

Upon arrival at the train station the author was greeted by two senior staff members attired in dark blue suits. (Incidentally, in almost any occupation in Japan "senior" almost always means older.) Within moments of arrival at the station we were whisked off in a chaffeur driven car to a nearby fashionable hotel where we enjoyed a sumptuous meal of shrimp tempura in a private dining room. After some preliminary discussion during lunch of probation services in Yamanashi prefecture, we departed for the mountains and a tour of the Suntory Wine Company's vineyards. We then settled down for more serious business. These preliminaries are recalled because they reflect both the graciousness of most Japanese and their preferences for conducting business. Most Western businessmen who have worked in Japan are on familiar terms with the Japanese penchant for mixing business with pleasure, whether it be enjoying one of Tokyo's expensive and glamorous nightclubs or playing golf at a company owned course. One Japanese colleague remarked to me one time, "all business gets conducted over drink in Japan."

Japanese probation officers, like their colleagues in other fields, were always hospitable and polite. They extended a friendly welcome, and they seemed to enjoy the attention they received from a visiting American scholar. Unlike in the United States where probation and parole are often in the public eye, they have a low profile in Japan. A number of probation officers stated that most Japanese citizens were unaware of the nature of their work and knew little, for example, about Rehabilitation Aid Hostels. My own discussion with Japanese friends confirmed this—few knew anything about the nature of probation and parole.

In addition to being friendly and polite, most officers provided candid and detailed responses to my inquiries. Overall, like the police that had been encountered during 1980 and 1981, the professional probation officers were a very impressive group. They seemed intelligent, thoughtful, hard working, honest, and they dressed neatly. They seemed intent on doing a good job.

It should be kept in mind that government service is highly respected in Japan, more so than is the case in the United States. This is particularly true of national service. Due to its prestige, it attracts talented applicants. Most Japanese acknowledge that the Finance Ministry is at the top of the list and M.I.T.I. also ranks very high. Further down the list is the Ministry of Justice and the National Police Agency. Both of the probation officers who hosted the Kofu visit had passed the National Public Service Exam and therefore were national governmental officials.

Yoshida-san was a slender man in his sixties while his colleague, Mr. Kasai, was a large man of similar age. Both proved helpful and considerate. Yoshida was in charge of the Liaison and Investigation section of the office while Kasai was the Chief of General Affairs. Both had worked in the Tokyo office before being transferred to this rural prefecture.

Responding to a question about the most serious problem they had to contend with, they noted that juvenile delinquency was on the rise, although the incidence remained low compared to urban areas like Tokyo. In their prefecture only Kofu itself was beginning to present an increase in juvenile offenses.

Discussing the organization and delivery of probation services, they noted that there was a liberal use of "day offices" requiring one day visits to outlying rural areas. Just twelve professionals staffed the office. Nine of the probation staff were line officers and they carried mixed caseloads as was customary all over Japan. Over 500 volunteers worked under the supervision of the professionals, providing a one to one ratio of staff to clients. But both administrators acknowledged the problem of the age gap between volunteers and parolees and noted that it was the single biggest problem they faced. There were just one or two under age 30 in the office.

Yoshida observed that he would like to interest more younger volunteers in joining but it was becoming increasingly difficult: "Young people today are more interested in their careers. All over Japan young people are more concerned for themselves and are not interested right now in helping with social problems" he claimed.

While the Big Brothers and Big Sisters (B.B.S.) movement, a program idea imported from America, had been strong during earlier decades and would have presented a natural recruiting ground for volunteer probation officers, interest in the movement had waned to the extent that it existed primarily on paper. The method of attracting V.P.O.'s to probation work was through word of mouth. Advertising was shunned as these probation officials were concerned that it "might attract the wrong kind of people." The day ended with the visit to the Yamanashi Itokukai (meaning "virtuousness") Rehabilitation Aid Hostel. It will be reported on in the chapter on halfway houses.

Chiba Visit

Chiba city is a very rapidly growing urban area near Tokyo and is consequently characterized by a transient population. As of March 1983 it was the most rapidly growing prefecture in Japan. Nineteen professionals worked out of the Chiba probation office and they had to contend with a rapidly increasing caseload. Professional staff to clients was one to 250, but as elsewhere the volunteers (1,211) handled direct service. Administrators in Chiba claimed that they were making a vigorous attempt to recruit younger volunteers and that a policy had been established in which only those 59 years old or younger were eligible to join. It was pointed out that the transiency made it even more difficult to recruit volunteers as neighborhood ties were very weak. Inquiring about caseloads, it was stated that while they were increasing, parole periods continued to be short — averaging just three or four months. The officers repeated the claim made by others, that they could be more helpful to clients if they had longer periods of time to work with them. It was also pointed out that longer parole periods allowed far better long term planning.

Discussing the major problem of employer resistance to hiring ex-convicts — a problem as widespread in Japan as in America — the director of the Chiba office stated that they had been engaged in a public relations campaign to win over employers through a series of talks and seminars. They claimed that they had employers in 30 different fields who were offering positions to released offenders. Granted, most were low level jobs. While probation officials all over Japan expressed concern for the problem of ex-offender employment, the fact of the matter was that many ex-offenders had some type of employment such as construction work.

One firm mentioned by a Chiba probation official was the Kasori Construction Company. Of the 300 parolees that were employed at that time, six worked for Kasori. Dry cleaning and food industries were other businesses that often hired ex-offenders.

Yokohama Visit

The visit to the Yokohama Probation Office featured an opportunity to observe three sessions between young offenders and the woman probation officer in charge of their cases. The setting was the "day office" in Yokosuka, in which officers conduct their business with volunteers and clients on a once a month basis. The probation officer was Ms. Konagai. She had studied at Kwanseigakun University, majoring in psychology. Ms. Konagai had recently participated in the 12 week international training course for Asian justice officials sponsored by the Japanese Ministry of Justice, and therefore spoke English fluently. English is the most commonly spoken language at the Institute's program and Japanese officials selected usually speak English fairly well.

After she had passed the National Public Service Exam, she had explored the probation service and found it appealing although she had also been in a position to accept an appointment at the Ministry of Labor. All three interviews were conducted in the presence of the volunteer officers assigned to their respective cases.

The first interview conducted by Ms. Konagai involved an 18 year old who had been glue sniffing. The Family Court had decided on probation for this first offense, but later the youth had assaulted his mother and he continued to sniff glue. The child had been born out of wedlock to a U.S. naval enlisted man who had returned to the U.S. The probation officer shared with me, without any expression of hostility but with a real sense of compassion for the youngster, the fact that there had been quite a few such instances since World War II, particularly near U.S. Armed Forces bases. She pointed out a fact with which the researcher had become only too familiar, half-castes are discriminated against in Japan. Japan's homogeneous society had erected a barrier against the employment of mixed racials. There would be other barriers as well. Marriage to a racially pure Japanese would be extremely unlikely. One could only feel sympathy for the plight of such a young person. Regardless of how he might struggle, his future seemed dim in such a society.

The young fellow had been enrolled in a private agricultural type of secondary school. While he had officially withdrawn, in actual fact he had been forced out because of poor grades, fighting with fellow students and frequent absences. He lacked the drive and motivation to seek employment, although he had briefly held a job before quitting. Like many other juvenile delinquents he behaved himself and acquiesced in the presence of his probation officer. However, he remained hostile and uncooperative with his older male volunteer probation officer—in this case a retired school teacher. The peer influence was powerful in his case and it contributed to his delinquency. Konagaisan remarked that his "minority complex" had seriously affected the boy's self-esteem and that his volunteer had been unable to effect any positive change. Bi-weekly visits had been arranged, but this schedule had not been adhered to and the previous month the youngster had stopped going to the volunteer's house. For two weeks during the preceding month he had worked as a waiter but his friends persuaded him to quit, claiming the job didn't pay much. Since there were indications that he was continuing to sniff glue the author inquired if he might be institutionalized for violating his conditions of probation. The probation officer responded that unless the evidence was clear the Family Court might refuse to take such action. However, after the volunteer and professional conferred they agreed that if his behavior didn't improve they would seek to have him placed in a training school. Konagai guessed that if he was sent to a training school, it would probably be for a period of from three months to one year. The probation officer noted that while his mother cared about the youth, she seemed impotent to assist him.

Another case involved a 17 year old probationer who was refusing to visit regularly with his volunteer probation officer. Inquiring about employment, the youth remarked that he had a part-time job in a snack bar. He had been in a minor accident with his motor scooter and displayed his scraped knee as evidence. Throughout both interviews the officer seemed authoritative and formal in her approach—taking the lead in asking questions. Asked about his daily use of time the probationer remarked that he did nothing. "I sleep until noon and then sometimes help my mother, but most of the time I'm home. Since I don't have a regular job, I can't get pocket money from my mother." The client's parents had been divorced; he lived with his mother, grandmother and older brother (also a probationer).

The client's volunteer was a 60 year old manager of a small company and at one point in the interview he interrupted to inquire about some of the youth's friends. He had previously shared little of this information, but in the presence of the probation officer he was more expansive. Throughout the session, the white sweat shirt attired adolescent sat in a docile, subservient posture with head bowed.

The ensuing discussion included the subject of his stimulant abuse and whether or not he was prepared to renew his agreement to meet regularly with his volunteer.

Later Konagai discussed his family background and prospects for the future. She noted that while he too was a high school dropout, he was healthy and didn't suffer a physical handicap like his brother who was also a probationer.

The third interview which was observed, but only briefly, involved the handicapped brother. Unlike his passive sibling, he sat defiantly with elbows on the desk as he faced Konagai. He was on probation for two offenses—glue sniffing and reckless driving. He responded in a vague and glib manner to most of the questions. As he had just become 20 years of age the Family Court judge had referred him to the public prosecutor for processing as an adult. He had been fined 100,000 yen (approximately $500) and placed on probation (according to his own statement) but a probation officer sitting nearby whispered that he might be lying. This terminated the final session observed.

A breakdown of caseloads handled by the entire Yokohama probation office is provided in Table 2.

Kyoto Visit

The Kyoto visit was more extensive than visits to the other cities mentioned previously. It was worked out in advance in Tokyo as were the other visits. Planning for visits to all locations had been undertaken with top administrators of the Rehabilitation Bureau of the Ministry of Justice during the first week of the research. The Kyoto portion of the field study, for example, had been roughly sketched out two months prior to arriving in that city in late August.

TABLE 2

Yokohama Probation Office Caseload — 1983

Source: Yokohama Probation Office, May, 1983

	Total of Yokohama P.O.		Yokusuka "Day Office"
Juvenile probationers	3483		
traffic		5060	86
long term	745		
short term	832		
Adult probationers	1241		43
Training school parolees	417		15
Prison parolees	385		11
	7103		155

Home conditions (Study or investigate family situation, job, inquiries etc. as *part of preparation plan for release*)

prisons	2320		55
training schools	278		
Probation officers including Administrators		36	
Active Volunteer Probation Officers		1683	(poss. 80% or 90% carrying a case)
Volunteer Probation Officers Authorized by Law		1830	
Probation area under Yokohama Office		42	"districts"

Average visits 14 per year at all Day Offices.

Throughout the entire period of the field study, the plans were always well coordinated. Officials placed no restrictions on requests.

Kyoto is the old capital city and is far more charming than Tokyo. It has the good fortune of being far smaller, with just 1.6 million inhabitants, than Tokyo with its 12 million plus population. With its many old temples and a lovely river that flows through the center of the city it is a popular tourist site for Japanese as well as foreign visitors. Like many Japanese cities it sits in a valley surrounded by mountains. On the famed Shinkansen, or Bullet Train, it is less than four hours from Tokyo.

Eighteen professional staff manned the office and the organizational chart resembled that of the Tokyo office. As in the other offices visited, a number of the professional staff spoke excellent English. This obviously aided the research as an interpreter was not required. One probation officer, a Mr. Yamaguchi, had conducted his own study of halfway houses in the United States. When asked what were the major differences between those in the U.S. and those in Japan he mentioned staffing. Japanese halfway houses typically do not employ professional people like social workers, psychologists, or psychiatrists but in America, he noted, there was usually at least one professional staff person involved, often a social worker.

On the first day at the Kyoto probation office the author was introduced to many of the professional staff and even had a brief meeting with the Director. This is an important ritual in Japan and although nothing of substance may be exchanged, it's a courtesy and common practice in Japan. On this day the director was absorbed in watching the annual televised nationwide high school baseball tournament. This summer event arouses as much interest in Japan as does the World Series in the United States, and therefore one could forgive him for being distracted on this occasion.

Later, during the first day, the author had an initial meeting with the five section chiefs of the office. After taking a seat at the corner of an oval conference table, the author immediately was asked to move and sit at the center across from the other staff. The Director seated himself at one end while the most senior probation officer positioned himself at the other end. The author was left with one side of the table to himself. Such positioning is important in Japan and there are unwritten rules regarding the seating of guests even in private homes.

As is the case in any country, dress reflects personality. Yamaguchi was an informal and friendly fellow in his early thirties. He wore an open necked shirt while several other staff wore short sleeved oxford shirts with ties. The Director was dressed in a gray suit with white oxford shirt and tie.

A Mr. Takahashi became the central figure in planning and coordinating my activities. A senior official, he had also studied some aspects of the justice system in the United States, primarily correction and probation services in New Jersey. He had an excellent command of English.

Some of the major issues facing the Kyoto office had already become familiar from contacts in other cities—too many older volunteers, not enough professionals, and budgetary constraints. Concerning the budget problem Takahashi commented, "The Rehabilitation Bureau was only organized 30 years ago and with its short history it is not so influential in competing for funds with the other bureaus. For example, the police can try to make their case on the basis of crime statistics, but our task is more difficult to accomplish."

One new bit of information learned from the discussions with Takahashi concerned the relationship of the correctional institution with the probation agency. First, he noted, when a person is received at the institution he is evaluated by a psychologist, which includes both testing and interviewing. Several of the tests used were to my surprise those that were developed in the United States—such as the Sentence Completion Test and the Wechsler Adult Intelligence Scale. It was difficult to understand why the Japanese had not constructed their own devices rather than relying on those from such a different cultural setting, but this seemed to reflect the commonly held notion that the Japanese are good at applications rather than more original work. In addition to a psychological evaluation, the inmate is required to submit to a vocational assessment and a social history. A report which includes these various sections is then simultaneously sent to the probation office and parole board. The probation office then makes available a copy for the volunteer assigned to the particular case. Once that report is received by the volunteer, he or she will interview the family of the offender and this written analysis will be sent back to the probation office with copies to the correctional institution and parole board.

Probation officials in Kyoto claimed that their branch of the Big Brothers & Big Sisters movement still was viable. It had 167 active members who engaged in a variety of activities with probationers and parolees. Activities included camping, hiking, bowling, skiing, cycling or sometimes just chatting at coffee shops. Some of the young men and women who are members of B.B.S. were urged to join by their parents who worked as Volunteer Probation Officers.

On a different topic the author inquired about the treatment of white collar offenders and was told that their numbers were few and of that group most were paroled.

On one occasion in Kyoto, a discussion with a group of professional and volunteer officers was held. Initially, my questions were directed at the volunteers—three older adults. The two women appeared to be in their sixties while the man appeared somewhat older. Asked about their relationship with young offenders, the older gentleman responded by stating, "In any field there is a generation gap. I do experience it with young parolees. I try to understand this younger generation, but they are brought up in an affluent society. They don't have the commitment to society that my generation felt. Therefore, I am anxious for the future of Japan. Concerning my cases, some are drug abusers. Most of the juveniles, who are abusers, do it for amusement. A few persist in their use and they become chronic. We have no effective treatment for it."

At this point the question was raised about group sessions and the use of ex-offenders in drug treatment programs, a commonly used technique in programs in the U.S., like Daytop and Synanon. The Japanese seemed a bit surprised at this. Takahashi noted that the law would probably prohibit the use of ex-drug abusers in the treatment of drug addicts. He acknowledged, however, that AA had taken root in the mid 1970's and that some of these groups had formed throughout Japan. For the most part the Japanese appeared to be relying on medical treatment for drug abusers, sometimes offered by psychiatrists.

This group discussion ended by Mr. Shimizu, a probation officer, commenting that he had enjoyed some success in the group counseling of some young drug abusers in a small community north of Kyoto. "Initially they were shy and reluctant to talk about themselves, but in later sessions they expressed real feelings. They were isolated and lonely and they had problems with their families. Many had stopped studying at school. They felt failure and it was compounded by a lack of acceptance from their peers at school."

These were some of the highlights of the field study conducted in Kofu, Chiba, Yokohama, and Kyoto.

TRAINING, EDUCATION AND CAREER PATTERNS OF PROBATION OFFICERS

There are three ways of becoming a probation officer in Japan. The first is to pass the National Public Service Exam and become eligible for an appointment in a variety of national agencies, depending on one's score. For example, the Ministry of Finance (if one is exceptionally able) and the National Police Agency might be possibilities. Competition on this exam is very severe, but once having passed it and accepted an appointment, one is on the "fast track." Usually, only graduates of top universities pass this exam—perhaps just ten are appointed annually. Opportunities will occur that will be denied to others. For those ten who are accepted, they are officially designated probation officers within six months.

A second method of entrance is offered if you are a college graduate (4 year or 2 year institutions). Today, most entrants are college graduates, but a few are high school graduates who have worked their way up from clerical positions. Typically, it takes four years for college graduates to be appointed probation officers. High school graduates take the primary exam and after working in a clerical capacity may be able to become probation officers in ten years.

Training courses for probation personnel are presented in Table 3. The *primary* course is for all newly appointed probation officers. The *secondary* course is taken after a few years with emphasis on practical aspects of the job. The *special* course is available to seasoned officers with the emphasis on "treatment," and the *senior* course is offered to those who are expected to assume supervisory responsibilities. The *supervisory* course is for "section chiefs" and upper level management.

TABLE 3

Training Curricula for Professional Probation Officers

Source: Ministry of Justice, 1983

	1983 Primary course	1980 Primary course	Secondary course	Special course	Senior course	Supervisor course
Number of trainees:	32	32	28	28	25	15
Categories of subject and number of hours:	96	84	45	6	54	9
Laws, regulations and procedures of probation, parole aftercare and pardons						
Laws and legal procedures	42	36	—	—	6	—
Criminology	12	12	—	—	9	—
Behavioral sciences	39	45	6	15	—	—
Counseling; casework	66	63	27	54	21	—
Case study	21	15	—	—	—	—
Introduction to the function of relevant agencies	7.5	13.5	27	—	6	—
Administration and staff management	—	—	—	—	9	42
Liberal arts	12	12	—	—	9	—
Field work and visits	84	102	10.5	6	9	3
Others	31.5	34.5	9	12	24	6
Total of hours	411	416	124.5	93	147	60
(days)	(92)	(87)	(15)	(20)	(32)	(13)

Note: The secondary course is organized and carried out at each parole board. Number of hours differs from board to board. The figures for the secondary course in this able how the average.

Training for V.P.O.'s is offered by the Rehabilitation Bureau and includes orientation at the time of appointment, advanced training for those serving their second and third terms, and various other ad hoc seminars. The response of V.P.O.'s to training is very mixed, according to officials, and many are absent at training sessions.

For those on the "fast track," special educational opportunities exist. The National Personnel Agency sponsors a fellowship program for civil servants that allows those who hurdle the demanding exam to engage in research and/or study for up to two years. In 1982, a recipient attended the University of Pennsylvania and in 1983 a probation officer attended Stanford University. The same agency also offers a short term program for six months, but again an exam is required.

Hitachi offers a three month fellowship to a probation officer each year. The "fellow" is free to develop his or her own program.

Career patterns of those who have passed the National Public Service Exam (the author shall refer to them as the "elite") mirror those in other public agencies, like the National Police Agency. A long term generalist type of training is characteristic. It is reflected in both varied assignments and geographical moves around the country. A brief look at the careers of two elite officers follows:

Hagiwara, known as "Haji," studied social work from 1964 through 1968 at college. The year he graduated he passed the National Public Service Exam and he and four others commenced their careers. He received on the job training and participated in the primary course. He then worked out of Osaka for three years. Afterward he was sent to a three month training course in Tokyo, which included study of criminology, sociology, and psychology. Hagiwara was then reassigned to Osaka for two more years. His next appointment was to the headquarters of the probation service, the Rehabilitation Bureau in Tokyo, where he worked in the General Affairs section with responsibility for personnel matters. From 1975 through 1979 he was assigned to the Research & Training Institute for the Ministry of Justice where he engaged in research on various "criminal trends." During this period his work took him to Canada and the United States. On one occasion he spent six months in the United States. Following this period he spent several years in Rome with the Ministry of Justice. Finally, he was appointed to the staff of the United Nations Far East Institute in Fuchu. While no longer under the auspices of the U.N., this Ministry of Justice training agency offers two annual courses to justice personnel throughout Asia.

Kakisawa studied sociology and attended Nagoya University. Afterward he passed the National Public Service Exam. Only seven were appointed in the elite program that year. From 1973–78 he worked as a probation officer in Nagoya. From 1978 through 1982 he worked in Osaka, first in the "supervision" section for three years and then for one year in "aftercare." In 1982, he was shifted to the Rehabilitation Bureau in Tokyo where he was the Unit-Chief in charge of Rehabilitation Aid Hostels throughout the country. He continued to serve in the post during the period the author interviewed him in 1983.

Briefly sketched below are the career patterns of ten other officials who were working out of the Rehabilitation Bureau, the equivalent of headquarters, during 1983. Perhaps the most salient issue is the geographical moves required of these officials.

K.S. born in 1936

1960 Shizuoka Probation Office, Probation Officer
1963 Rehabilitation Bureau (Supervision Division, Supervision Unit) Secretary
1967 Rehabilitation Bureau (Supervision Division, Parole Unit) Unit-Chief
1968 Rehabilitation Bureau (General Affairs Division, Legal Affairs Unit) Unit-Chief
1971 Sendai Probation Office (Liaison Section) Section-Chief
1972 Tohoku Regional Parole Board (Liaison Section)Section-Chief
1975 Urawa Probation Office (Liaison Section) Section-Chief
1976 UNAFEI, Faculty Member
1979 Rehabilitation Bureau (Supervision Division) Assistant Director
1981 Rehabilitation Bureau (Liaison Division) Assistant Director
1982 Rehabilitation Bureau (General Affairs Division) Assistant Director
1983 Rehabilitation Bureau, Counselor (Related to legal matters; drafting of legislation for consideration by the Diet)

S.S. born in 1927

1957 Sendai P.O. Probation Officer
1959 Saga P.O. Probation Officer
1962 Fukuoka P.O. Probation Officer
1964 Rehabilitation Bureau (General Affairs Division, Legal Affairs Unit) Unit-Chief
1968 Rehabilitation Bureau (Liaison Division Survey Unit) Unit-Chief
1969 Kinki Regional Parole Board (Liasion Section) Section-Chief
1972 Fukuoka P.O. (Supervision Section) Section-Chief
1975 Research & Training Institute of Ministry of Justice, Instructor
1978 Utsunomiya P.O. Director
1980 Kinki R. P. B. Secretary-General
1982 Rehabilitation Bureau (Supervision Division) Director
1983 Rehabilitation Bureau (Liaison Division) Director

K.I. born in 1928

1953 Tokyo P.O. Probation Officer
1961 UNAFEI Faculty Member
1968 Rehabilitation Bureau (General Affairs Division) Assistant Director
1970 Rehabilitation Bureau (Liasion Division) Assistant Director
1972 Research & Training Institute of M. J., Researcher
1975 Tokyo P.O. (Supervision Section) Section-Chief
1977 Tsu P.O. Director
1979 Kinki R. P. B. Board Member
1980 Rehabilitation Bureau Counselor
1983 Rehabilitation Bureau (Supervision Division) Director

S.I. born in 1938

1961 Sapporo P.O. Probation Officer
1965 Hokkaido R. P. B. Probation Officer
1971 Research & Training Institute of M. J. Assistant Researcher
1974 Sapporo P.O. (After Care Section) Section-Chief
1976 Sapporo P.O. (Liaison Section) Section-Chief
1978 Kanazawa P.O. (General Affairs Section) Section-Chief
1980 Nagoya P.O. (Supervision Section) Section-Chief
1982 Rehabilitation Bureau (Liaison Division) Assistant Director
1983 Rehabilitation Bureau (General Affairs Division) Assistant Director

M.M. born in 1939

1964 Kanto R. P. B. Probation Officer
1965 Rehabilitation Bureau (General Affairs Division Legal Affairs Unit) Secretary
1968 Tokyo P.O. Probation Officer
1977 UNAFEI Faculty Member
1980 Meabashi P.O. (Supervision Section) Section-Chief
1983 Rehabilitation Bureau (Supervision Division) Assistant Director

K.K. born in 1951

1976 Corrections Bureau (General Affairs Division) Secretary
1977 Immigration Bureau (Immigration Examination Division) Secretary
1978 Civil Affairs Bureau (Third Division) Secretary
1979 Rehabilitation Bureau (Pardon Division) Secretary
1080 Osaka P.O. Probation Officer
1983 Rehabilitation Bureau (General Affairs Division Legal Affairs Unit) Unit-Chief

One final observation: it's interesting to note that writers like William Ouchi (author of *Theory Z*) in discussing Japanese management in the private sector, describe generalist training programs in which managers are often shifted from post to post. The same appears true for managers in the public sector. Law enforcement administrators have career patterns that are generally similar to the probation administrators identified above.

REFERENCES

Bartollas, C. *Introduction to Corrections*, New York: Harper & Row Publishers, 1981
McCarthy, B. R. and McCarthy B. J. *Community-Based Corrections*, Monterey, California: Brooks/Cole Publishing Company, 1984
New York Times. "Strict Probation Praised in Georgia," *The New York Times*, May 6, 1984, p. 39.
Sasaki, K. "Probationary Supervision." Unpublished paper, United Nations Asia and Far East Institute for the Prevention of Crime and Treatment of Offenders, 1983.

Shelden, R. *Criminal Justice in America: A Sociological Approach.* Boston & Toronto: Little Brown and Company, 1982.

Smykla, J. *Probation and Parole,* New York: Macmillan Publishing Co., 1984.

Tokyo Probation Office, "Profile of the Tokyo Probation Office." Unpublished mimeographed statement, 1983.

Whitehead, J. "Burnout in Probation Officers: Results of a Survey," paper presented at the Academy of Criminal Justice Sciences Conference, Louisville, Kentucky, 1982.

CHAPTER VI

Volunteers in
Probation/Parole

UNQUESTIONABLY, THE LARGE scale use of governmentally appointed volunteer probation officers (V.P.O.s) is the most unique feature of the Japanese system. While it is true that there are a variety of volunteer programs in the United States, and that the overall number of volunteers have significantly increased in the last decade, they are not organized nationally nor on such a grand scale as in Japan. Therefore, it is this issue, more than any other, which distinguishes community-based corrections in Japan from that of the United States. Before offering a detailed look at the Japanese approach, a few words about the role of the volunteer in the United States seem appropriate.

Historical Sketch

Historically, volunteer programs in corrections had their roots in England almost 200 years ago (McCarthy & McCarthy, 1984). Prisoner visiting programs were organized by John Howard and Elizabeth Fry. Fry commenced her activity with incarcerated women in London's Newgate Prison in 1813. Appalled at the degradation and misery of the women, she practically singlehandedly sought to correct abuses. Coming along somewhat later in the United States was The Philadelphia Society for Alleviating the Miseries of Public Prisons and the Salvation Army. They were among the early groups in the United States that visited imprisoned men and women. During this same period, volunteer organizations developed in Massachusetts, New Jersey, and New York.

As mentioned in an earlier chapter, John Augustus was the first American volunteer to become involved in probation and parole activities. He inspired others to contribute their energies to helping ex-offenders but eventually professionals took over the field

(McCarthy & McCarthy, 1984) and the role of volunteers waned.

In more recent times, Judge Keith Leinhouts is credited with reviving the volunteer movement in this field. His Royal Oaks program generated national interest because of its impact on recidivism rates. One study found that the probation volunteers' efforts in the Royal Oaks program resulted in a recidivism rate of less than half that of a comparable group that did not rely on volunteers. The judge's efforts led to a number of other states adopting the idea and the operation eventually became affiliated with the prestigious National Council on Crime and Delinquency. Called Volunteers in Probation (V.I.P.) the concept was extended to volunteers in prison and parole.

The American Volunteer

An underlying recurrent issue throughout this study has been the problem of caseload size. The ratio of professional workers to clients in both nations has been outrageously high. In Japan the ratio was 1 to 205 during 1981, while the ratio was approximately the same in the United States. For example, during 1982 the ratios for several U.S. cities were as follows: New York City 1 to 180, Detroit 1 to 150 and Los Angeles 1 to 360 (Parker, 1983).

There are three main arguments for the use of volunteers—cost effectiveness, enhancing agency public relations and benefits for the offender (Shields, Chapman, & Wingard, 1983). The first argument is the most prevalent in the fiscally conservative climate of the 1980's. With the huge ratios of offenders to professionals, volunteers are potentially able to make a major contribution at a variety of levels. As Shields, Chapman, and Wingard (1983) point out, "well managed volunteer programs are a strong public relations strategy." This is important in a context in which probation and parole services are misunderstood and a skeptical public receives nightly sensationalized media accounts of criminal behavior. Undoubtedly, the most important issue though is delivery of services—do clients benefit from the involvement of volunteers? As in Japan, the unpaid volunteer is often viewed less skeptically by the offender than is the paid worker. In theory, it is because the person is offering help, merely because he or she wants to.

Because of the many jurisdictions within the United States, approaches to the use of volunteers vary tremendously from region to region. In some instances they provide auxillary services which include transportation, recreation, and assistance on special matters such as budgeting. In other instances, they offer friendship and support to the offender—in effect providing the basic relationship that overworked parole officers are unable to provide.

Schier and Berry (1972) have identified ten general roles that volunteers may play in the United States:

1. Support, friendship, someone who cares and will listen
2. Mediator, facilitator of social-physical environment (get jobs, intercede with teacher, open up opportunites, run interference wth system)
3. Behavior model, just be a good example
4. Limit setting, social control, conscience
5. Teacher-tutor in academic, vocational, or social skills
6. Observation, information, diagnosis, understanding, extra eyes and ears on the probationer, on the community, or even on the agency on behalf of the community.
7. Trainee rather than trainer; intern preparing for a career in the criminal justice system
8. Advisory or even decision-making participation in formulating policy
9. Adminstrative support, office work, and related facilitation
10. Help recruit, train, advise, supervise other volunteers

Contemporary Volunteer Efforts

In 1979, one study estimated that in the overall field of corrections more than 350,000 persons were involved in 4,000 volunteer programs. While more than half were women, a sizable minority (43 percent) of men were involved (National Council on Crime and Delinquency, 1979). Eighty one percent were white and 84 percent had received formal education beyond high-school. While a little less than half had been working for two years or more as volunteers, the majority were new to volunteerism. Among the current programs nationwide, several are described below.

The Volunteer Probation Officer Program in Lincoln, Nebraska has received high marks from the U.S. Justice Department, according to McCarthy & McCarthy (1984). It emphasized a precise matching of volunteers with offenders and relied on a careful screening of applicants. Furthermore, it included a well conceputalized training program. Directed at youthful "high risk" offenders, its original purpose was to offer the young person a structured and intensive learning experience. Later, it was expanded to the elderly. The program lasts for a year. The first two months involve counseling by probation officers and participation in court operated educational classes. A volunteer is then assigned with an eye toward the matchup of the person's skills, resources, and interests with that of the offender.

Results of research conducted indicated that offenders in the experimental group committed 46 percent fewer offenses than persons in the regular probation program. While 55 percent of the volunteer counselor group committed new offenses during the probationary year, 70 percent of the control group committed new offenses.

One interesting program operated in California is the Volunteers in Parole program offered by attorneys (Cohn, 1983). The director of the program, Steve Cohn, stated that young people on parole are matched with attorneys who "volunteer to help the parolee through the re-entry period." The idea is for the volunteer and parolee to share recreational activities, for the attorney to occasionally assist in finding employment, housing, etc. The goal is to build a relationship of mutal trust and respect. Both parties agree to work together for at least one year. As Director Cohn stated in personal correspondence:

> Not all the relationships work out well, and, at times, people have to be rematched. I would say the success rate of the relationships is evenly divided between great impact, moderate impact and minimal impact on the course of the parolees' post release behavior.
>
> As our goal is to establish a friendship, we feel it is important that the supervisional duties of the parole agent and the supportive efforts of the attorney-volunteers are kept distinct and separate. In that way, the parolees feel freer to confide in their volunteer.

More than 100 attorneys volunteered for the program between 1980 and 1983, with the average age being in the 27 to 35 years of age range. This last point is particularly noteworthy when comparing the U.S. system wth the Japanese one. Perhaps the major weakness of the Japanese approach is that the average age is 60 years.

Connecticut has a rather well developed program (Connecticut Office of Adult Probation, 1983) for volunteers. Volunteers are active in all 20 of its field offices. The program is administered by a supervisor of volunteer services and six coordinators. Volunteers are expected to spend from one to four hours a week with each probationer for the entire period of probation.

For 1982, there were 142 who started service, while 78 completed their 12 month service. Most of Connecticut's volunteers are college educated. Their occupations varied greatly from white collar professional, like a psychologist, to blue collar factory workers. The average age of Connecticut volunteers was identified as mid-forties by one staff person. Again, this is in contrast with the much older group in Japan. Finally, for 1983, the annual report stated that of the 120 cases, 78 (66 percent) were considered successful. Success was defined to mean a case usually produced "some type of change, whether social and/or attitudinal during the probation period."

JAPAN'S VOLUNTEER PROBATION OFFICER

In contrast to the great variety of programs and roles played by volunteers in the United States, in Japan they are organized nationally and they provide the bulwark of services to clients. They are the front line service and provide the direct day to day counseling of most probationers and parolees. In 1981, 46,935 volunteer probation officers served throughout Japan, compared to just 797 professional officers. As noted earlier the ratio of professional officers to offenders is 1 to 205, not unlike the situation in the United States. However, with the inclusion of volunteers, a one to one ratio exists between a worker and an offender. In fact in the Tokyo office in 1982 the ratio was 1.0 to 0.8.

While the Japanese system, with its army of volunteers, allows for close working relationships between volunteers and offenders, professional probation personnel are not always happy being relegated to supervisory, consulting, and coordinating roles. Some of the professionals would like to be at the grassroots level themselves and occasionally grumble that they could do a better job than the volunteers when it comes to counseling and direct service. Of course, as noted earlier, a handful do operate out of the "Direct Treatment" Unit of the Tokyo office. But it cannot be denied that the virtue of the system is being able to draw on the large cadre of volunteers.

Another important feature is that volunteers, in addition to being non-official, are local, living and working in the same community as their charges. Of course, this same point would apply to American volunteers in most instances.

In Japan, community based services were reorganized around 1949 and thought was given to creating an all professional corps of officers, as in other countries like England and the United States, but two considerations prevailed. First, government officials generally had a strong commitment to the use of volunteers in a variety of social welfare areas, which included programs for offenders, but secondly, funding was lacking at that time. The volunteer Probation Officer Law of 1950 officially defined the mission of the V.P.O. as follows:

(i) Helping persons who have committed criminal offenses to improve and be rehabilitated at the same time;
(ii) Changing public opinion for the prevention of crime; and
(iii) Cleaning up the community.

Qualifications for volunteers were spelled out as follows:

(i) To have confidence and support of the community with respect to one's character and conduct;
(ii) To have enthusiasm for probation work and time for such work;
(iii) To have financial stability;
(iv) To be healthy and active.

Tables 1, 2 and 3 provide some data on the age, years of experience, and occupational background of volunteers in the Tokyo office. As the tabular data reveals, in addition to housewives, many Buddhist and Shinto priests, along with businessmen, volunteer their services as V.P.O's. Officially they are appointed by the Minister of Justice upon the recommendation of the Director of the Proba-

TABLE 1
Age of Volunteer Probation Officers (Tokyo)

Source: Tokyo Probation Office January, 1983

Under 30	2	(0.1%)
30 - 39	63	(1.7%)
40 - 49	495	(13.1%)
50 - 59	1,412	(37.3%)
60 - 69	1,188	(31.3%)
70 and Over	625	(16.5%)
Total	3,785	(100.0%)

TABLE 2

Years of Experience of Volunteer Probation Officers (Tokyo)

Source: Tokyo Probation Office January, 1983

less than 2 yrs.	....	938	(24.8%)
2 - 4 yrs.	....	357	(9.4%)
4 - 6 yrs.	....	302	(8.0%)
6 - 8 yrs.	....	267	(7.0%)
8 - 10 yrs.	....	247	(6.5%)
10 - 15 yrs.	....	673	(17.8%)
15 - 20 yrs.	....	476	(12.6%)
20 - 30 yrs.	....	345	(9.1%)
30 and Over	....	189	(4.8%)
	Total	3,785	(100.0%)

tion Office, after having been screened by a Volunteer Probation Officer Selection Council. He or she is then in the capacity of a public official working without remuneration. Volunteers are appointed for two years, but many are reappointed, as Table 2 demonstrates. Of the 3,785 who worked out of the Tokyo office on January, 1983, 1,009 were women.

Tanigawa (1982), like many probation officers, scholars and others interviewed, raised the problem of too many older volunteers (see Table 1). He noted that one of the reasons for the older age of volunteer probation officers is the retirement system in Japan—often people retire at 55 or 60 and some then move into volunteer work. Tabular data on volunteer probation officers in the Tokyo prefectural office mirrors that found elsewhere in Japan.

Interviews With Volunteer Probation Officers

In addition to observing volunteer and professional officers at work with clients, arrangements were made to interview several volunteer probation officers away from the line of fire—in their homes.

One volunteer interviewed, a Mrs. Shibata, was in business with her husband, who owned and operated an international trading company, importing English woolens. They were visited at their stylish condominium in Tokyo. This gray haired women, in her

TABLE 3
Occupations of Volunteer Probation Officers (Tokyo)

Source: Tokyo Probation Office, 1983

Agriculture, forestry & fishery	275	(7.3%)
Industry	289	(7.6%)
Commerce	558	(14.7%)
Service entrepreneurs	129	(3.4%)
Construction	64	(1.7%)
Firm employees	142	(3.8%)
Civil servants	162	(4.3%)
School teachers	83	(2.2%)
Company executives	355	(9.4%)
Medical doctors	59	(1.6%)
Religious priests	351	(9.3%)
Practicing lawyers	18	(0.5%)
Estate agent, owner	129	(3.4%)
Social workers	119	(3.1%)
Housewives	475	(12.5%)
Others	156	(4.1%)
No occupation	421	(11.1%)
Total	3,785	(100.0%)

50's, was well dressed and socially poised. Almost immediately she produced her medal, awarded to her by the Minister of Justice, and stated that "before you can get this you have to get local awards—usually it takes 20 years before you can receive this, but I received it after 16 years." Several probation officers had indicated that one problem with volunteers was that they were too connsumed with the idea of seeking medals as opposed to offering service to clients. On the other hand, there might be a touch of jealousy in this argument voiced by professional officers—they are not eligible for such awards. Akira Tanigawa (1982), the former Director-General of the Rehabilitation Bureau, offered a different point of view on the subject:

> Public recognition of course is a strong inducement for people to become and remain VPOs. The Emperor, Minister of Justice and other officials at various levels of government regularly award in

formal ceremonies certificates for meritorious service as VPOs. However, whether formal recognition in such ways counterbalances personal financial detriment is a matter subject to debate. (p. 333).

At the time of the interview, Mrs. Shibata carried one client, but there had been times when she had carried three simultaneously. She noted, "Initially I tell them I cannot give them money or be a guarantor." She commented on her current case, a 21 year old male:

When he was a minor he violated traffic laws with his motorbike—traveling without a license. He was put on probation. After that there was no trouble with the law. One month ago he was released from probation and while helping with his father's business he engaged in theft with three others. They stole from a woman who was working at a Turkish bath (in Japan, women who work at such establishments are often prostitutes). He was put on probation again—this time it will be for four years. This fellow is a weak person and when he is with his friends he will show off. The group can prod him into doing something like that. Most of the time he is quiet and docile. I've tried to talk to him about his problems, but I'm low key. He seems like a kind person.

Asked why the judge had appeared to be so lenient with her client on this second offense, she replied, "probably he took his total record into account. His thefts had been very minor." An inquiry about the process for dealing with probationers and parolees who violate their conditions led to this comment:

You should know that when a person commits a serious offense, after having left an institution, the professional probation officer makes the recommendation to the parole board. They have the final decision. If a person violates parole regulations, but doesn't violate the penal code, he or she can be returned to prison directly wthout an appearance before a judge. Undoubtedly you know that parolees cannot keep company with *boryokudan* (organized crime) and that they must maintain an established residence. Leading a transient life could be a violation.

The previous case she had dealt with involved a 32 year old male convicted of smuggling marijuana:

He was quite bright and single. At the time he was working in Manila, teaching Japanese at a small private school. From wealthy parents, he enjoyed a university education at a good school. In order to start a small business, he asked his parents for money. They declined, so he looked elsewhere. About three years ago he established friendship with some shady characters in Manila who were tied to some kind of criminal organization. Although he himself did not directly smuggle marijuana he let them use his name on packages. This fellow was not worldly and got sucked in. He was imprisoned for three years. The parents were moralistic and refused to take him in after his release, and therefore I had to be a 'go between'. They offered no financial support, but I went to negotiate with them to see if he could get a little money to make a start. It was tough and I argued for at least 50,000 yen. They agreed as long as I took responsibility for the loan. But I also took the opportunity to tell them that it was their responsibility for having created a person like this. Before one can effectively intercede in a case like this you have to bring the parties together. One thing I did, and I admit it was a bit of a show, was to scold the son in front of his parents. Today he is still paying back the loan while he works in the printing business. He's off parole and occasionally drops by.

Another volunteer, a man by the name of Yoshioko, was umemployed at the time and lived on the outskirts of Tokyo in a traditional old Japanese wooden house. Previously he had worked as a tailor. His family had lived in some type of structure on that plot of land for more than three hundred years. Tall, slender, and wearing sandals, he received the researcher in the living room where little cakes and tea were served on a steamy summer afternoon. Yoshioko carried three juvenile cases at the time and had worked for seven years as a volunteer. Asked to discuss a case, he mentioned a young rapist he had counseled:

The fellow was 20 years old and was sent to prison for three years on a rape charge. There was also extortion involved. Once in prison he assaulted four persons and that added 1 yr. 4 mos. to his sentence. He was released on parole after three years, one month. The family was pretty decent, but the father was strict, the mother was tolerant. The older brother worked in a manufacturing plant. He was the youngest and there were three sisters. One sister was a fashion model, whom he felt close to and who was active in show business. The young man was arrested around the time his mother developed mental problems and was hospitalized. The sister tried to take care of both of them along with the stress of her own life. She couldn't handle it, became depressed and took her own life. My young parolee always felt he didn't get enough attention. Although he was an excellent student in elementary school, he was just average by junior high school. Academically he was not able to get into the public high school of his choice so he had to go to a lower class private school. This defeated him. He lost his will to study. After high school he worked at a Sushi restaraunt, but at the time of the crime was unemployed. While he was in prison, the sister committed suicide. The parents were undecided as to whether to tell him. I went to the prison to talk with officials about the problem [author's note: it is typical for volunteers initially to get to know their clients before they are released from confinement] . It was one of my early contacts, and I told him the truth. Prison authorities had lied, informing the offender that his sister was busy working. I felt like a "confidante" with him. His adjustment since prison has not been easy. There was depression after his sister's death and he felt responsible for it. Because he felt responsible, he matured and has held a job. In prison, he learned accounting and works at that trade now, in an office heading up a section that includes 15 people. While in prison, we exchanged letters and I sent him several books to read.

The author inquired as to whether Yoshioko found the work frustrating. "It's not too frustrating. I'm like a traffic signal, but you can't be too harsh on clients or they'll leave. Sometimes if a person had been convicted earlier or had received tougher discipline, he wouldn't have committed offenses, but you can't correct the situation by using those methods. You have to develop a trusting relationship in which the client will open up to you with his innermost secrets."

Finally, asked if offenders received money upon discharge, Yoshioko noted that a person can make a little money while in prison. Typically, a person may leave with 20,000 yen ($83) in his possession, but for some who have been incarcerated for 10 years or more they might leave with 300,000 yen ($1,250) in their possession.

Both Shibata and Yoshioko impressed one as talented individuals who seemed highly committed to their work and who appeared able to get positive results in most instances.

REFERENCES

Cohn, S. "One-On-One: The Volunteers in Parole Programs" and personal correspondence, San Francisco: Bar Association of San Francisco, Barristers Club of San Francisco, and the State Bar of California, 1983.

Connecticut Office of Adult Probation, "Handbook Volunteer Programs," Connecticut State Judicial Department, 1983.

McCarthy, B. R. and McCarthy, B. J. *Community Based Corrections*, Monterey, California: Brooks/Cole Publishing Co., 1984.

National Council on Crime and Delinquency, *Volunteers in Probation*, Royal Oaks, Mich.: National Council on Crime and Delinquency, 1979.

Parker, L. C. "Japan's Volunteer Probation Officer System Offers Cheap but Viable Approach to Reform." *The Japan Times*, Op-Ed Page, August 21, 1983.

Schier, I. H. and Berry J. L. etal., *Guidelines and Standards For the Use of Volunteers in Correctional Programs*, Washington, D.C.: Law Enforcement Assistance Administration, 1972.

Shields, P. M., Chapman, C. W., and Wingard, D. R. "Using Volunteers in Adult Probation," *Federal Probation*, Volume 47, No. 2, 1983, pp. 57–64.

Tanigawa, A. Chapter 18, "Public Participation and the Integrated Approach in Japanese Rehabilitation Services," in *Criminal Justice Asia: The Quest for An Integrated Approach*, United Nations Asia Far East Institute for the Prevention of Crime and Treatment of Offenders, 1982.

CHAPTER VII

Halfway Houses

HALFWAY HOUSES IN THE UNITED STATES

THE ORIGIN OF the earliest halfway houses is unknown, but some writers have suggested that they emerged in response to Christian charity (McCarthy & McCarthy, 1984). In 1817 in the United States, a recommendation for the establishment of a halfway house appeared before the Pennsylvania legislature. In the previous year a riot in a Pennsylvania prison prompted the legislature to establish a commission to study prison problems and suggest reforms. However, the proposal never went into effect as it was believed that ex-inmates would provide a bad influence on one another.

Halfway houses were started in 1820 in Massachusetts in order to provide food, shelter, and various services to released offenders. Various private citizens continued to develop facilities throughout the balance of the century. One facility, the Isaac T. Hopper Home was developed by the Quakers in 1845, and is still in operation today.

The halfway house movement, after experiencing a decline in the first half of the 20th century, began to pick up steam in the early 1950's. Following on the heels of "disenchantment with the rehabilitative potential of the prison" (Smykla, 1981, p. 158) and the emerging view that a community link was necessary between prison and the community various halfway houses began to sprout.

The author's personal interest in halfway houses goes back to 1961–62 when, as a graduate psychology student, he had interned at one of the first group of facilities for federal offenders in the United States and later was employed at the one in Brooklyn, New York as a counselor. Under the auspices of the Federal Bureau of Prisons, the Attorney General, Robert Kennedy, started up four

"Pre-Release Guidance Centers" for young offenders given early release from confinement. The centers were opened in New York, Chicago, Los Angeles, and Detroit.

While not having a control group for comparison, Kennedy (1961) nonetheless, reported encouraging results. Citing data on recidivism, he claimed that of the 300 young men sent to the centers and later released on parole, less than 25 percent had violated their conditions of parole. This was a good batting average. Later, the centers were to change their name and be called Federal Community Treatment Centers (CTC) (Beck, 1979), but their basic purpose of assisting ex-offenders to readjust in the community remained the same. A later more sophisticated study of the effectiveness of these 14 centers resulted in a finding that the clients had better employment records during the early months after release than did control group members. However, the author (Beck, 1979) also reported "there was no evidence indicating that overall offenders referred to CTC engaged in criminal activity less often or that their criminal activity was less serious. There was data, however, which showed that offenders most likely to commit a new crime may engage in less criminal activity if referred to a CTC."

As these reports suggested, readjustment in the community, recidivism and employment were three of the commonly used criteria to assess effectiveness. Cost was and continues to be a key factor for obvious reasons. Researchers invariably point out that the per capita cost of maintaining a person in a halfway house is considerably less than incarcerating an individual in prison. This is true in Japan as well as in the United States.

Shelden (1982) has noted that there are three principal assumptions about the value of halfway houses over incarceration: they are less costly, they are more humanitarian, and they enhance the rehabilitative potential of offenders. While grudgingly acknowledging that the first two assumptions are probably valid, he believes the third assumption is incorrect. He claims that research has failed to support the view that they are superior to incarceration in reducing recidivism. Noting the fact that both community based programs for drug addicts and ex-offenders are often in crime ridden areas of cities that suffer from urban decay, he rightly asks how such community settings are capable of helping these individuals.

One example of a comprehensive type of halfway house program is the one operated by the Safer Foundation (*The New York Times*, 1983). Job placement was a key factor and Safer's results have been positive. Officials of the Iowa and Illinois inmate organization reported that only 10.9 percent of the ex-offenders treated recidivated within two years, which they noted was just one-third the national average. Since 1970, more than 42,000 ex-offenders have been assisted by the organization. Their clients received intensive counseling by professionals and volunteers. The approach of the centers stressed "taking pride in being responsible for one's own actions and success." Basics were offered in the form of food, shelter, medical assistance, legal counsel, and help in obtaining low-cost housing. "Safer" clients also received help with reading, writing and mathematics, but as already noted, jobs were vital. One staff member stated, "If we can place them within 15 days, there is a 100% less chance of their going back."

In a later report on employment and placement of residents of Community Treatment Centers (CTC's), Beck (1981) noted that the findings of a study of 2,108 released offenders were promising. Release through the centers was found to significantly improve postrelease employment success for both white and minority parolees. Specifically, through the federally sponsored Community Treatment Centers it was found that offenders had less unemployment, more days worked, and more money earned compared to inmates released directly into the community from prisons. Curiously, minority offenders who passed through the CTC's had reduced recidivism rates while whites did not. As Beck (1981) suggests, it appears that minorities benefited most because of the greater disadvantages they confront in gaining employment.

Smykla's (1981) view on the value of halfway houses in reducing recidivism is more positive than Shelden's. Basing his statement on 55 evaluative studies, he commented. "In terms of recidivism, there is evidence that appears to support the statement that halfway houses do succeed in reducing the recidivism rates of former residents in comparison to ex-offenders released directly into the community" (Smykla, 1981, p. 167).

In general, a great variety of programs in the U.S. have used the label "halfway house." Some have been small, secure community-based institutions that provide a full range of services while others have been loosely structured programs that provide shelter but little else to ex-offenders (McCarthy & McCarthy, 1984). As these authors point out, one of their main advantages, which is often overlooked, is that they provide a sufficiently secure environment to protect the community. Clients' activities and associations are typically monitored and support services, role models, and recreational pursuits are available. Under this kind of supervision, the residents of these programs should be less likely to engage in criminal behavior than if they were released directly on their own, with or without conditions of parole.

HALFWAY HOUSES IN JAPAN

Overall, the goals of halfway houses for released offenders in Japan are similar to those of the United States. However, the organization of programs, policies, and staffing are vastly different. But even these differences pale alongside the contrasts in culture. In Japan they are known as Rehabilitation Aid Hostels.

A brief sketch of the history of Japan's halfway house movement was offered earlier in Chapter IV, so the author shall therefore move to a discussion of the contemporary period. One of the top administrators in the Rehabilitation Bureau of the Ministry of Justice, Kazuhisa Suzuki, was selected to work with the author and arrange the field study. Correspondence wth Suzuki-san laid the groundwork for the initial meeting at the Ministry of Justice during the first week in Tokyo. Like many Japanese higher echelon officials, he had been rotated through a variety of assignments and geographical locations during his career as a probation official (see Chapter V for Career Patterns of Officials, including Suzuki). At the time of the interview, he was the third ranking official in the Rehabilitation Bureau. He spoke English fluently and seemed eager to help. During that time in his career when he was a faculty member at the United Nations Far East Institute in Fuchu, he had authored a paper entitled "Halfway Houses in Japan" (Suzuki, 1978). He kindly updated many of the statistics to 1982, and some of the data cited in this chapter have been drawn from that paper. In his overview article on the role of halfway houses, he noted that their origin stemmed from "disillusionment with traditional correctional institutions as a means of rehabilitation, together with the humanitarian concern for the treatment of offenders." Much later as probation and parole evolved as alternatives to incarceration, it was recognized that halfway houses offered a third choice for offenders who required more than "occasional meetings with probation officers." In Japan, a halfway house placement came to be associated with the needs of chronic offenders who had "deep rooted personal disorders." That policy continues today. As mentioned earlier, older repeat offenders in Japan are often shunned by their families upon their release from prison. They often have no choice but to accept lodging at a Rehabilitation Aid Hostel.

The number of halfway houses in Japan, along with the daily population of these residences, has declined in recent years as Table 1 illustrates. Some hostels have been permanently closed while others have temporarily suspended operations. Overall capacity has been reduced by almost one-third over the past two decades. Furthermore, there have been dramatic decreases in the daily populations of these facilities since the peak period of 1959. A gradual increase in the accomodation rate can be observed since 1974, but many vacancies remain and probation officials do not anticipate any marked increase in the foreseeable future.

The field study of halfway houses included interviews with administrators and not infrequently they expressed their concern for the economic viability of their programs. While the individual per capita subsidies have increased over the years, in 1982 hostels received daily allowances of just 1,692 yen ($7.05) for room and board or 674 yen ($2.80) for room only. In addition, 1,265 yen ($5.27) was provided for general management and miscellaneous expenses per resident per day. The subsidies from the national government would be sufficient to pay hostel workers a wage equivalent to that of probation officers only if the accomodation rate reached 80%, but in fact it has only been around 55% in recent years as Table 1 showed. Therefore, it is understandable why some facitlites are struggling to survive.

A profile of an average halfway house reveals the following breakdown on *expenditures*: personnel 42.5%; services, foods, and workshop expenses 43.9%; office expenses 3.4%; depreciation 3.3%; and construction and repairs 6.7%. For *income* the following percentages apply: national government subsidies 50.3%; workshop income 20.6%; donations and local government subsidies 12.3%; property divided 6.0%; resident contributions 6.8%; other 4%.

Keiwaen Rehabilitation Aid Hostel (Half-Way House)
For Juveniles — Tokyo

Shin Kokai Rehabilitation Aid Hostel (Half-Way House)
For Adult Males — Tokyo

*Seiwakai Rehabilitation Aid Hostel (Half-Way House)
For Adult Males — Tokyo*

Honganji Bya Kosso Rehabilitation Aid Hostel (Half-Way House) For Adult Women — Author and Staff — Kyoto.

TABLE 1

Rehabilitation Aid Hostels in Japan 1958–81;
Number of Hostels, Daily Population and Accomodation Rate

Source: Japanese Ministry of Justice, 1983

Year	Number of Hostels	Total Authorized Capacity	Average Daily Population	Accomodation Rate (%)
1958	150	3,921	2,900	74
1959	158	4,130	3,061	75
1960	156	4,122	3,120	76
1961	151	4,076	3,089	76
1962	152	4,153	3,016	73
1963	148	4,114	2,780	69
1964	144	4,106	2,560	64
1965	137	3,721	2,325	60
1966	132	3,464	2,215	61
1967	130	3,374	2,122	63
1968	127	3,510	1,946	56
1969	125	3,545	1,765	50
1970	121	3,389	1,675	50
1971	114	3,322	1,557	47
1972	113	3,303	1,466	45
1973	108	3,178	1,407	45
1974	104	3,072	1,354	45
1975	103	2,972	1,449	49
1976	103	2,856	1,456	50
1977	103	2,805	1,483	52
1978	103	2,792	1,470	52
1979	101	2,787	1,449	52
1980	100	2,645	1,441	53
1981	100	2,617	1,437	55

What is the reason for the decline in the use of halfway houses? Conversations with administrators around the country point to the economic upsurge of recent decades. With more plentiful job opportunities, more offenders have been able to live more independently. Granted, most of the jobs have been unstable positions requiring only manual labor. A glimpse of the type of work engaged in by ex-offenders residing in halfway houses is offered later in this chapter in the description of the hostels visited. Regardless of the level of employment, larger numbers of parolees have been able to live on their own (with the approval of their parole officers, of course) or minimally they have been able to leave hostels at an earlier stage in the readjustment process.

Another feature of the hostel movement that has contributed to their declining numbers is the problem of continuity of owner ship. In an earlier period, a particular person may have been in spired to set up a halfway house for reasons of charity, but wha about his or her successors? The spirit of public service has wanec in Japan over the past 20 years and some facilities have closed for this reason. Although many hostels are incorporated into foundations, typically the foundation consists of just the land and building donated by the founder.

In reviewing data on the facilities and staffing of hostels it should be noted that most are small facilities—more than 70% have capacities between 11 and 30 individuals.

Most hostels today, as Table 2 reveals, cater to both adults and juveniles. Justice officials acknowledge the problem of mixing juveniles with adults but point to economic considerations and the problem of offering services in sparsely populated areas. Often they are located in prefectural capital cities with few being available in outlying areas or local communities.

For the past two decades the government has supported the reconstruction and in some cases, the expansion of facilities. Organizations such as the Japan Bicycle Promotion Association and the Japan Shipping Promotion Association have been major contributors in this effort. Still, few facilities have air conditioning or central heating plants. Table 3 provides data on the physical characteristics of the halfway houses. Note that construction materials have changed dramatically since 1960 when most buildings were wooden. The standard on room space is just 3 square meters per resident according to the Ministry of Justice regulation and therefore it is common for hostels to have rooms of 9.9 square meters (6 tatami mats) per three residents. (See photos of various hostels which provide both external and interior views). While Japanese

TABLE 2

Capacity of Hostels, 1982

Source: Rehabilitation Bureau, Ministry of Justice, 1983

Type	Male only	Capacity	Female only	Capacity	Male & Female	Capacity	Total	Capacity
Adult only	24	(658)	1	(10)	2	(40)	27	(708)
Juvenile only	7	(132)	1	(14)	-	-	8	(146)
Adult & Juvenile	62	(1,675)	4	(54)	1	(22)	67	(1,751)
Total	93	(2,465)	6	(78)	3	(62)	102	(2,605)

Table 3

Physical Characteristics of Hostels, 1960-1982

Source: Rehabilitation Bureau, Ministry of Justice, 1983

Construction of Facilities	1960	1967	1972	1977	1982
Wooden houses	96.5	69.1	36.3	30.3	22.9
Concrete block buildings	1.4	9.3	8.7	11.6	12.3
Concrete & steel buildings	2.1	21.6	55.0	58.1	64.8
Total	100%	100%	100%	100%	100%
Total floor space (sq. m)	69.044	59.649	64.734	60.908	58.427
Floor space per authorized capacity	15.9	15.6	19.4	20.8	22.5

are used to living in close quarters, with few people having a room to themselves, administrators would like to be able to allocate more space per resident. Overall, the housing standards for halfway houses are probably no different than they are for the average Japanese, according to Suzuki (1978).

Tables 4 and 5 provide information on the characteristics of personnel employed by the hostels in 1982. Many of the personnel have extensive experience in working with offenders before they have entered halfway house employment and many took positions after retirement. The average age of these workers (see Table 4) gives a clue to the fact that many are retired. Suzuki claims that the average monthly pay is low by Japanese standards and that long working hours—typically 12 hours per day—and the self-sacrifice required make recruiting young and able personnel a difficult task. Also, he notes, it is reflected in the morale of currently employed staff. Some are enthusiastic while others are not.

Curiously, the majority of staff come from occupational fields totally outside social service and criminal justice. This may reflect

Table 4

Staffing of Rehabilitation Aid Hostels, 1982

Source: Rehabilitation Bureau, Ministry of Justice, 1983

Staff members	Number	Pensioners	Average age	Average monthly pay
Director	58	37	64.1	133,995 yen ($558)
Director concurrently Chief guidance worker	44	25	59.6	163,371 yen ($680)
Chief guidance worker	59	35	61.2	124,555 yen ($519)
Guidance worker	149	63	54.4	108,674 yen ($453)
Clerical staff	37	3	47.6	87,445 yen ($406)
Cook	81	19	56.0	77,662 yen ($324)
Vocational instructor	29		47.7	188,182 yen ($784)
Total	467		56.3	119,054 yen ($496)

Note: 240 yen = $1

Table 5

Previous Careers of Rehabilitation Aid Hostel Staff, 1982

Source: Rehabilitation Bureau, Ministry of Justice, 1983

Previous Occupation	Director	Director chief guidance worker	Chief guidance worker	Guidance worker
Police Agency	7	6	2	5
Court or Prosecutor's office	2	0	0	0
Correctional Instituion	14	10	19	21
Probation Service	6	9	33	5
Education	3	4	1	4
Social Welfare	0	1	1	2
Others	25	16	32	89
Total	57	46	58	126

on the low pay and long hours. Furthermore, it suggests that hostel employment cannot compete for highly qualified people. On the other hand, it might imply that there are not professionally trained or educated people available for this type of work.

Legally, authorities are not allowed to order probationers or parolees to live at hostels for a specified period. A hostel placement is made upon the request of an offender and justice officials acknowledge that this undercuts the "treatment" feature of these facilities because it reduces control. Under the law for the aftercare of discharged offenders the following individuals are eligible for a Rehabilitation Aid Hostel placement:

1. A person who has completely served his sentence of imprisonment with or without forced labor or penal detention.
2. A person whose execution of sentence of imprisonment with or without forced labor or penal detention has been excused.
3. A person who has been granted suspension of execution of sentence to imprisonment with or without forced labor and whose sentence has not yet become final.
4. A person who has been granted suspension of execution of sentence to imprisonment, with or without forced labor, but has not been placed under probationary supervision.

One probation official complained that in theory the probation office could entrust the residential care of probationers or parolees to selected private individuals, but regulations required that only hostels could be used for this purpose. Therefore, by implication, this policy would seem to have the effect of blunting any imaginative efforts to arrange housing for offenders.

Another problem faced by probation officers is the limit on aftercare services. Although probationers and parolees are eligible for admission to hostels while under supervision, other categories of offenders are eligible for only six months residence after discharge from penal institutions. The types of offenders residing at halfway houses in 1982 are revealed in Table 6. Data on the length of stay at hostels are offered in Table 7. While most offenders terminate their living arrangements with hostels with the consent of the staff (66.2%), a significant percentage depart without notifying

Table 6

Types of Offenders Residing at Rehabilitaion Aid Hostels, 1982

Source: Rehabilitation Bureau, Ministry of Justice, 1983

Category of offenders	Number of offenders	
Parolees from prisons	4,708	(43.8%)
Adult probationers	507	(4.7%)
Parolees from training schools	394	(3.6%)
Juvenile probationers	210	(2.1%)
Offenders released upon expiration of Prison term	3,795	(35.4%)
Offenders discharged on suspended prosecutions	684	(6.4%)
Offenders discharged on suspended sentences	433	(4.0%)
Total	10,732	(100.0%)

Table 7

Length of Stay at Hostels, 1982

Source: Rehabilitation Bureau, Ministry of Justice, 1983

Period of Stay	Number of Offenders	
under 4 days	1,201	(15.7%)
5 to 9 days	687	(9.0%)
10 to 19 days	836	(10.9%)
20 to 30 days	893	(11.7%)
31 days to 60 days	1,499	(19.6%)
61 days to 90 days	859	(11.2%)
91 days to 180 days	1,127	(14.7%)
181 days to 1 year	431	(5.6%)
1 year and over	123	(1.6%)
Total	7,658	(100%)

the staff (20.8%). Not surprisingly, the interviews with halfway house staff confirmed that those who left prematurely, or without the consent of staff, were more likely to return to prison. Nationally, during 1982, 4.2% of residents were discharged for failing to obey house rules, 4.0% were rearrested or taken into custody for more serious infractions, 4.8% left for "other reasons."

The Research and Training Institute of the Ministry of Justice has conducted a number of studies on those placed at halfway houses and in research conducted in 1980, Ito, Seta & Hagiwara, reported on the characteristics of 1,480 residents, 97.6% of whom were males. The sample was made up of 81.9% who were released from prison. Of those, 17.8% had been imprisoned six times or more. Often they had been convicted of theft or fraud. Prior to being imprisoned, nearly 50% had worked at unskilled day labor jobs, including factory work. More than half had changed jobs four times or more, a very high number in a country famous for its lifetime employment policy. Regarding marital status, just 40.7% had been married or had cohabited with a member of the opposite sex. One third of the offenders had less than 5,000 yen ($20.81) in their possession at the time they arrived at the hostel. Consistent with interviews conducted at the hostels in 1983, most residents had some type of employment (89.6%) in 1980. The survey found that morale among the ex-offenders was reasonably high, but that various problems (particularly drinking) not infrequently resulted in their violating the rules of the hostel. Many of the hostels have rules concerning meals, cleaning, curfew, etc. Usually the drinking of alcoholic beverages on the premises is prohibited, but occasionally it is allowed if it is done in the privacy of one's room and does not interfere with the activities of others. Also, typically there are rules against betting, fighting, stealing, etc.

Economically, those who stayed longer at the hostels usually fared better. For example, among those who had saved 200,000 yen, 10.1% had been in residence for more than five months, but the number went up to 22.7% for those in residence over eight months.

This 1980 study concluded by citing data on recidivism. Statistically, the authors noted, the probability of recommitting an offense was 81.1% for those who stayed one month or less, but it became just 40.9% for those who stayed from eight to nine months. As noted earlier, these findings are consistent with the reports of staff offered during interviews at halfway houses.

In a later 1982 report by the same authors, they found that not only was length of residence at halfway houses correlated with reduced recidivism rates, but that the trend was true even for those who had nine convictions or more. Factors that correlated with reduced recidivism included amount of savings, age, and length of hostel residence.

For those residents who have worked out mutually agreed upon terminations and appear ready to re-enter the community, it is not uncommon for their new employers to arrange housing. For 1982, the Ministry of Justice reported that 1,767 (23.1%) offenders worked out such arrangements. Also, 1966 (25.6%) took up residence with family members or relative, while 1,507 (13.8%) rented their own housing. Social welfare agencies provided lodging for 162 (2.1%) individuals, while 748 (9.8%) made other arrangements. The whereabouts of 1,958 (25.6%) former hostel residents was unknown to Ministry of Justice officials.

On Site Visits To Halfway Houses

Interviews and observations were made at seven Rehabilitation Aid Hostels in Japan and the data gathered helped to supplement the information obtained elsewhere. Quite often the interviews yielded knowledge that had already been acquired, but occasionally something new emerged. This portion of the study focused on those new bits and pieces of information that helped to flesh out the overall study of Japan's halfway house movement.

The following hostels were visited: *Shinkokai* (Tokyo), *Keiwaen* (Tokyo), *Seiwakai* (Tokyo), *Yamanashi Itokukai* (Kofu), *Chiba-Ken Kiseikai* (Chiba), *Honganji Byakkoso* (Kyoto) and *Ikusekai* (Kyoto). As of July 1983, 17 hostels existed in the Tokyo area. The *Shinkokai*, *Seiwakai* and *Deiwaen* hostels in Tokyo were among those first visited. The first two are for adult males, while the third was for juvenile males. Nakamura-san, the Chief of the Aftercare Section of the Tokyo office, accompanied the author on these three visits. He was friendly and receptive to all questions. In his late 40's, he had been assigned to the Tokyo area just one year earlier.

On the drive over to the hostel from the probation office Nakamura was asked about national or regional meetings of hostel directors and staff members. He replied that the directors of the 17 hostels in the Tokyo area met five times a year but that operational staff from the different programs met once a month. This is reminiscent of the Japanese penchant for forming associations and organizations, an outgrowth of the general emphasis upon groups in Japan. Nakamura commented that recently the meetings for operational staff had rotated around all of the Tokyo area hostels with staff of the host facility offering detailed descriptions of their programs.

The *Shinkokai* hostel was the first visited. An attractive building constructed in 1968 to replace an earlier facility on the same plot of land, it was tucked between some other houses in an outlying urban area of Tokyo near *Ikebukuro* (see photos). Like most Japanese housing, it had virtually no land surrounding it.

The director of the hostel had been in charge of it for many years, having taken it over from his father. Let's call him Shimada. Earlier he had been unable to devote much time to it as he had been in the banking business. Shimada had retired as president of a local bank. This pleasant, white haired man and his wife extended typically gracious Japanese hospitality and were receptive to all inquiries. Not surprisingly, with his background, he was well prepared with numerical data on the *Shinkokai* operation.

Most residents were adult parolees, but several were under a "suspension of prosecution" arrangement. Asked about the employment status of the current residents, the director noted that "it's difficult to find employers willing to accept ex-offenders. Employers feel apprehensive that these ex-offenders will be a bad influence on other workers. The construction industry is our main employer, but some small businesses and shops will hire our residents." At that time all 27 residents of the hostel were employed in the following occupational areas: construction (10), unskilled factory work (10), truck driving (2), pipeline construction (2), restaurant and food business (e.g. assistant cook) (3).

Discussing the accomodation rate, the director stated, "there are some rural hostels in Japan that have been forced to close, but not in Tokyo. We run about 80% capacity and can accomodate 40 men."

Asked about the kinds of problems he faced with residents, he explained that while consumption of alcoholic beverages was prohibited on the premises, occasionally a resident would get drunk while outside the facility and cause a problem in the neighborhood. Rarely did ex-offenders commit new offenses while in residence at the hostel, he explained, but occasionally after they left, when they were more vulnerable and lonely, they ran into trouble. Some types of ex-offenders were not accepted at the facility, including members of *boryokudan* (organized crime members), arsonists, those with psychiatric problems, drug abusers and rapists.

One of the older staff members explained that while the neighbors tended to accept the facility because it had been there for many years, if new construction was attempted a public outcry would occur.

Akira Tanigawa (1982), the Director-General of the Rehabilitation Bureau in 1982, offered a case study example of the hostility of the community toward a halfway house:

> Rehabilitation Aid Hostel A was established as a private programme in 1898 and was incorporated in 1954. When it first opened on its present site it was surrounded by uninhabited farmland and forests distant from residential areas. In 1980, the

hostel planned a complete reconstruction of its facilities and an expansion to accomodate 30 rather than 20 male adult and juvenile offenders. The hostel's neighbours reacted highly negatively to the proposed expansion plan and insisted that the hostel be closed down and removed from the neighbourhood because it had become a source of constant unrest. In May, 1980, the hostel was forced to sell approximately half the tract of land upon which it stood to finance reconstruction, and then began to tear down its old building. Community representatives demanded a meeting with representatives of the hostel to negotiate the matter, and presented 17 demands which included measures to prevent nuisances in the neighbourhood which might be created by hostel residents. In July, a statement in opposition to reconstruction, signed by 14 local residents, was submitted to the hostel and filed with the local probation office and mayor. The principal stated basis was that hostel residents had committed more than ten offenses, for which they had been arrested by police, within the preceding five years, a circumstance that had created great anxiety about and fear of crime among inhabitants of the neighbourhood. The mayor and probation staff urged upon the petitioners the importance of reintegrating offenders into the community, but were rebuffed by the residents, who warned they would obstruct reconstruction physically if it were not cancelled.

In October, representatives of the hostel association decided to relocate; in December they selected a site elsewhere in the suburbs of the city, located 500 metres from the nearest private residence. When construction of the new building began in March 1981, surrounding residents in the new location began their own campaign against construction. Staff members of the local probation office and hostel tried in the course of two meetings with the residents to convince them that construction should proceed, but both meetings broke up with rancor All efforts to convince persons living in the neighbourhood and the public at large that the project should proceed ended in complete failure and in May 1981 construction was suspended, and remains so today. Both parties are in the process of requesting the mayor to mediate the dispute. (p.333)

Over a lunch of tempura at a nearby restaurant in Ikebukuro, Mrs. Shimada, the director's wife, who had worked in the field for 24 years, explained a little of the daily routine. "In general," she noted, "we try to offer an informal, family type of life. We pay attention to the diet and meals offered, The *Futon* (Japanese sleeping mattress) is kept clean. We try to put ourselves in the shoes of those staying here. We don't formally do counseling but we extend ourselves to the residents. Often they come to us for assistance."

She mentioned that she got up at 5 a.m. and that breakfast was served at 6:30. At 10 p.m. a roll call was taken. Asked about residents who weren't back by 10 p.m., she replied, "as long as they call and let us know, it's okay."

The *Seiwakai* hostel for adult males was slightly larger, accomodating up to 60 residents. It was also a clean, relatively new facility located on the outskirts of Tokyo. The director, Mr. Osasa, explained that while the location was in a lower class area of the city, the ex-offenders felt comfortable with it and that local neighborhood residents were not critical or particularly sensitive to the existence of the hostel. As in the case of the *Shinkokai* halfway house, the current operator had inherited it from his father. The man who originally built the facility had a motto "to build savings through trust," meaning that for residents to accumulate savings one first had to be trusted by an employer. The founder had built the original structure with his own funds.

Describing the atmosphere of *Seiwakai* Hostel, one staff member offered "we try to see things through the eyes of the other person. Although they're ex-offenders they require our respect as human beings and they appreciate our effort to understand them."

Concerning employment, all 27 residents were employed at that time, one third in construction work and another third in a small business operated through the hostel. The workers of this business cleaned and maintained local streets and parks. One staff member pointed out that two other Tokyo area hostels operated their own businesses. In one case, a hostel baked bread for school lunches, while another sold dairy products to local people in its area.

Asked about the most frustrating part of his job, the director stated, "of course, the relationships with residents. Some claim they don't know their role here and they expect us to take care of them. It's a kind of dependency problem. Also, we have a few who break house rules on drinking, etc."

Discussing adjustment problems in the community the director continued,

> In this business, ex-offenders are most likely to commit new offenses when they are unemployed. Also the family is a factor. When these men have been imprisoned once or even twice, their

families may accept them back, but after that they are more reluctant. The offenses may even be relatively minor ones, but repeated offenses will lessen their chances. At that point the ex-offender will drift away from his family and the hostel staff will not press him to reestablish those ties. Of course when it comes to new relationships most will hide the fact that they are ex-criminals. We don't have research data on this, but the staff generally believes that our residents may easily initiate new relationships, but they frequently are terminated at an early stage. There is less stability in lower class neighborhoods like this one. Curiously, those who have committed offenses such as fraud and theft are less likely to develop enduring relationships than those who have engaged in robbery and murder. Some of these latter mentioned offenders have done very well. For example, some have constructed their own houses. Perhaps in some cases those with longer sentences feel a deeper sense of repentance.

Near *Nakano* train station in Tokyo is the newly opened Keiwakai Rehabilitation Aid Hostel for young male offenders. Tanaka-san, a congenial man in his 70's, greeted us upon arrival. He was in charge of this facility, an attractive new building that reminded me of a small Japanese inn, sometimes called a *Minshiku* in Japan. During introductions he mentioned, without apparent bitterness, his imprisonment by American Armed Forces during World War II. He related the now familiar problems of hostel management including "too much Saké drinking" on the part of residents. Tanaka shared the discussion with a younger assistant, Shimizu, a man in his late 20's. Both were modestly attired and wore open shirt collars. Explaining their roles, Tanaka mentioned that he and his wife were like houseparents as opposed to being professionals. The Bicycle Promotion Federation had generated most of the funds for the new facility, which had a capacity of 20. In addition to the three above mentioned staff, *Keiwakai* employed a cook. Most residents came from training schools, although a third were on probation.

It was explained that the residents who were over 15 were working at that time, but that they would return at 5 p.m.—they could not legally be employed for more than 8 hours a day. Most of them obtained jobs through the efforts of Mr. Shimizu and Mr. Tanaka, but a few managed to secure their own positions.

Tanaka commented "when the young men seek out their own jobs, I am the head of a boarding house as far as references are concerned. It is necessary because most Japanese do not appreciate the plight of these youngsters. Some community organizations are supportive, but individuals are usually not sympathetic."

Asked to expand on the difficulties faced by himself and the rest of the staff he said, "some of these young men try to adjust, but at the same time they feel guilty about their prior delinquency and this makes it difficult for them. They also have low self-esteem."

Tanaka sketched a recent case as an example.

> We have a boy who was sent to a juvenile training school for glue sniffing. He was self-destructive, lost weight and had poor eating habits. His mother had a history of psychiatric problems and while his father was not indifferent he seemed unable to raise the youngster on his own. After he left junior high school, he got into trouble. But now, since he's been here, things have improved. He found a job with a transportation company working as an assistant to a driver, loading and unloading. When he applied for the job he gave my name, but told the employer I was a relative. Maintaining a good adjustment, he hopes to get his license and become a driver at a later point. Previously, before being sent to the training school, he changed jobs every week. Although he's doing well now, we believe he's not ready to be thrown on to his own. It's possible for someone like him to stay here until 20 years of age.

The interview terminated with a brief discussion of discipline at the *Keiwakai* hostel. A 10 p.m. curfew was in effect for all residents, alcohol within the house was prohibited but a little drinking outside was tolerated. Residents were required to be polite to their peers and to staff members. Smoking was tolerated, but not encouraged.

Chiba-Ken Kiseikai was founded in 1899 by Buddhists. The director, a former probation officer, explained that their fundamental belief was that people are born good and they remain so, although they may occasionally sin. While they may sin, if they return to the spirit of what they were at birth, they will be fine. However, the director was quick to point out that the hostel now had no religious connections. Like the other facilities it was modern, clean and offered very attractive accomodations. Figure 1 presents the floor plan for this hostel. The Chiba prison, adjacent to *Chiba Ken Kiseikai*, sends some of their parolees to this halfway house although they accept ex-offenders from a variety of institutions.

A Mr. Okuyama was in charge. He explained that they had very few rules and that they did not wish to "smother" released offenders in a regimented atmosphere.

> Historically, there was a huge gap between the rich who offered charity to ex-offenders and the recipients themselves. Ordinary citizens didn't play much of a role in offender programs, but after World War II things changed and the vast wealth of those who had offered charity to ex-offenders was gone. Also, another problem exists. Today, at the community level, people are self-centered and they want to avoid involvement with ex-cons. They even resist when hostels try to rebuild. They say there is no need to bring in more ex-offenders. Here, we didn't have the problem because a hostel, along with Chiba Prison, existed on this site for many years before most people ever lived in this neighborhood. Furthermore, our staff and the prison staff live nearby. Along with the fact that we allow this facility to be used by the community for conferences, meetings, etc. it has encouraged a more receptive attitude on the part of the community.

Asked about the type of atmosphere at the house, Okuyama replied "our aim is to give as much independence as we can to each offender but also to make them aware of problem areas. After that, to return them to society as soon as possible."

Yamanashi Itokukai offered accomodations for adults and juveniles. Located in rural *Yamanashi* prefecture, in the city of Kofu, it was one of just several halfway houses available in the entire prefecture. At the time (August, 1983) there were several probationers, as well as parolees, housed at *Yamanashi Itokukai*. A Mr. and Mrs. Hando managed the facility. Several of the parolees had been at the hostel on earlier occasions. As an older man wandered by in the hallway, a staff member gestured and commented "some of the previous residents get along very well. That man's latest offense was driving without a license. He's been to prison nine times, paroled six times. Originally a painter, he has a low intelligence level and that may be part of the problem."

Inquiring about the most difficult problems faced by the staff Mr. Hando said, "selfish conduct, not adjusting to the group, sometimes drinking too much and occasionally fighting both outside and inside the hostel." This facility was clean and bright like the others visited, although it was a much older building.

The highlight of this visit was an interesting discussion about the change in social controls in Japan over the years. Curious about

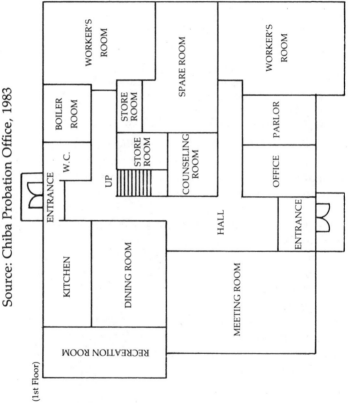

FIGURE 1

Floor Plan of Chiba-Ken Kieikai
Rehabilitation Aid Hostel
Source: Chiba Probation Office, 1983

(1st Floor)

(2nd Floor)

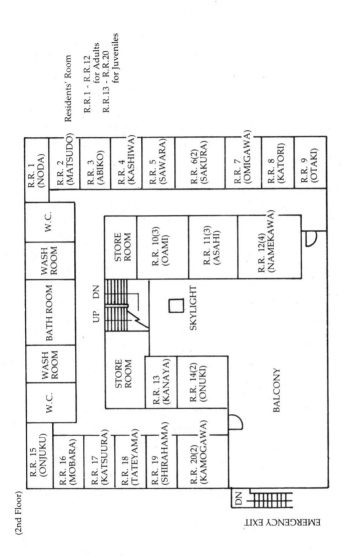

Residents' Room

R.R.1 - R.R.12
for Adults
R.R.13 - R.R.20
for Juveniles

R.R. 1 (NODA)
R.R. 2 (MATSUDO)
R.R. 3 (ABIKO)
R.R. 4 (KASHIWA)
R.R. 5 (SAWARA)
R.R. 6(2) (SAKURA)
R.R. 7 (OMIGAWA)
R.R. 8 (KATORI)
R.R. 9 (OTAKI)

W.C.
WASH ROOM
BATH ROOM
WASH ROOM
W.C.

STORE ROOM
R.R. 10(3) (OAMI)
R.R. 11(3) (ASAHI)
R.R. 12(4) (NAMEKAWA)

UP   DN
SKYLIGHT

STORE ROOM
R.R. 13 (KANAYA)
R.R. 14(2) (ONUKI)

BALCONY

R.R. 15 (ONJUKU)
R.R. 16 (MOBARA)
R.R. 17 (KATSUURA)
R.R. 18 (TATEYAMA)
R.R. 19 (SHIRAHAMA)
R.R. 20(2) (KAMOGAWA)

DN
EMERGENCY EXIT

changes in the types of criminal offenses committed, the author inquired about these trends. It was stated that glue sniffing and various types of stimulant abuse were far more common than they used to be. Also, that the juvenile who engaged in this activity did so out of "curiosity" not out of need—drug dependency was not the issue. It was explained that earlier, stronger social sanctions would have prevented much of this form of drug abuse, but that people were less disciplined today. Society had a more rigid code of conduct. This meant that a delinquent had a deeper and clearer appreciation of his misdeed and he was more apt to reform. In contemporary Japanese society with its eased restrictions on deviant behavior, a "double edged sword" existed. On the one hand it was explained, it was easier to rehabilitate a person because community sanctions are weaker (employers and relatives are more inclined to accept the offender back), but at the initial stage a person might be more inclined to risk a criminal offense (he or she may be less inhibited than before) than in earlier decades.

Finally, Mr. Hando noted that drug abuse had increased in part because *boryokudan* members, through their organized networks, had made drugs more available. The author's earlier experience with the police agency's frustration in curbing drug traffic supported Handa's observation.

In Kyoto, two hostels were visited with Toru Yamaguchi, a probation officer who had undertaken his own study of halfway houses in the United States. He had received a special grant through the Rehabilitation Bureau in Tokyo and been given a leave for that purpose several years earlier. A personable and informal young man in his mid 30's, he was enjoyable company. The *Ikuseikai* hostel for adult males in Kyoto city was the first facility we visited. Like the others, it was clean and pleasant. We were met by the entire staff of four older men and sipped green tea as we discussed their program. It had been founded in 1947. One of the workers, a Mr. Suimada, explained the approach

> The principle of this house is to engage in self-reflection. There is a meeting once a month to discuss their attitudes and problems. Those who behave well are rewarded by the staff in the form of goods—food and the like. The psychological atmosphere also includes the idea of confronting them with their problems in the day to day activities of the house. It might, for example, include mundane things such as keeping their rooms clean. Most of our residents are men in their 40's.

One thing seemed clear about what was offered by way of the psychological atmosphere at all the halfway houses visited. None claimed to offer the highly emotionally charged type of encounter and confrontation so characteristic of American programs like Synanon, in which a person might be forced to sit in the center of a group and be emotionally raked over the coals for some type of failure or misdeed. Also, none were staffed by ex-offenders.

During lunch with Yamaguchi, he briefly commented on his own research on U.S. halfway houses. He had visited 35 programs all over the country. One of the major differences he found was that many of the houses had one or two professional staff associated with it, often social workers with M.S.W. degrees, but more surprising to the Japanese probation officer was the fact that a high percentage (perhaps 80%) employed ex-offenders as staff members. That was unheard of in Japan.

Yamaguchi favored the creation, on an experimental basis, of a national government system of halfway houses, sidestepping the present system of government subsidies to privately operated houses.

The Nishihonganji Byakkōsō Hostel was the last one visited. A facility for adult women situated on the outskirts of Kyoto, it was sponsored by a large Buddhist sect. At the close of World War II, with rising crime rates accompanying the social disarray of the period, there were any number of women offenders (often with children) who lacked housing. Prison authorities were eager to have some type of short term residence to assist these needy women with the problems they confronted—food, shelter, and employment. The Nishihonganji Temple became aware of the problem and decided to establish a halfway house on its own property in Kyoto in 1950. While a fire in later years severely damaged the original wooden frame building, a new facility was constructed in 1969 with funds provided by the Japan Cycling Society, various citizens and Nishihonganji Temple. During the 1960's the program had a religious character, which included a required morning worship service.

Today, the hostel cares for women who are drug abusers or prostitutes. The plight of these wretched women was detailed by the male director. He commented, "many of the women work at night and have numerous opportunities to make contact with the drug world." He continued, "Our drug abusers are particularly difficult to rehabilitate. Many have come from poor families and have had emotional problems. They have had relationships with *yakuza* (organized crime figures) who offered them drugs and they have become dependent. They often get drawn back into that life after they leave. They're stigmatized, too. A concrete example: because of fuel costs, we can't afford our own private bath here and these women are forced to bathe in public facilities. With their *yakuza* tatoos exposed, they become humiliated—some leave. Because they're poor, they borrow money from others after they arrive. They can't pay back this loan, and sometimes this causes them much humiliation.

One could not help being touched by the picture that emerged. Under-financed, it sounded as though there were barely enough funds to provide basic food and shelter, never mind psychological treatment and a stipend to allow these women to get back on their feet. These women, caught up in an exploitative cycle with organized crime figures, seemed unable to find a way out of this seedy world.

The other three staff were women and they seemed warm and caring. One split her duties between the hostel and the temple itself, which was located in a different part of the city. Later she was to appear in a black robe when the author was treated to a private tour of the impressive temple grounds.

The average age of the ten women was 45 years, although one juvenile was in residence at the time of my visit. Four worked as housemaids, one worked in a kitchen at a hospital, one worked in a department store, two worked at hotels, and one worked at a little shop nearby. Some had been paroled from a Womens Correctional Institution but some were there under a "suspended execution of sentence."

This completes the field study of halfway houses.

REFERENCES

Beck, J. L. "An Evaluation of Federal Community Treatment Centers," *Federal Probation*, Volume 43, No. 3, September, 1979, pp. 36–39.

Beck, J. L. "Employment, Community Treatment Center Placement, and Recidivism: A Study of Released Federal Offenders." *Federal Probation*, Volume XXXXV, No. 4, December, 1981.

Ito, H., Seta, O. and Y. Hagiwara. "Study on the Characteristics of the Residents of Treatment Programmes in Rehabilitation Aid Hostels." First report and Third Report, *Bulletin of the Criminological Research Department*, Research and Training Institute, Ministry of Justice, 1980 and 1982.

Kennedy, R. F. "Halfway Houses Pay Off." *Crime and Delinquency*, Volume 10, January 1964, No. 1, pp. 1–7.

McCarthy, B. R. & B. J. McCarthy, *Community-Based Corrections*, Brooks/Cole Publishing Company, Monterey: California, 1984.

New York Times. "Group Finds Gain in Rehabilitation." *The New York Times*, Sunday, October 2, 1983, p. 30.

Powers, E. "Halfway Houses: An Historical Perspective," *American Journal of Correction*, 21, July-August, 1959.

Shelden, R. *Criminal Justice in America: A Sociological Approach*. Boston & Toronto: Little Brown and Company, 1982.

Smykla, J. O. *Community-Based Corrections: Principles and Practices*, Macmillan Publishing Co., Inc., 1981.

Suzuki, K. "Halfway Houses in Japan," unpublished manuscript, United Nations Asia Far East Institute for the Prevention of Crime and Treatment of Offenders, 1978 (amended for the author, 1983).

Tanigawa, A. Chapter 18, "Public Participation and the Integrated Approach in Japanese Rehabilitation Services," in *Criminal Justice Asia: The Quest for an Integrated Approach*, United Nations Asia Far East Institute for the Prevention of Crime and Treatment of Offenders, 1982.

CHAPTER VIII

Conclusion

JAPAN'S PROGRAMS TO rehabilitate ex-offenders appear to have enjoyed a modicum of success and seem to be superior to those of the United States. However, given stiff community resistance, they have fallen somewhat short in terms of their ability to arrange good jobs. True enough, most ex-offenders seem to have found some type of employment in the boom economy that has lasted over the past decade, but these positions have been, by and large, unskilled jobs, what Americans call "dead end" jobs. They aren't the types of positions that fit into the "permanent employment" scheme so widely heralded in the United States.

While probation officials understandably grumble about the skimpy budgets they have to work with, from a different perspective, one could say it's "rehabilitation on the cheap." Of course, the reference is to the volunteer probation officer system which costs very little.

Scholars' Criticism

Most of the data gathered for this research project have emerged from the field study and with interviews of people working within the system, but what about professionals and scholars outside the system? Several that were interviewed offered a quite different perspective. Interviews with these three scholars were extremely helpful in obtaining a fuller picture of the strengths and weaknesses of Japan's programs in this field.

Perhaps the person with the best grasp of the issues, large and small, that was interviewed in the entire study was Kyoko Iwata. She enjoyed the benefit of many years of experience in probation before retiring from the field in 1980, but she continued to be familiar with later developments. While studying for her master's degree in social work at the University of Hawaii, she had become fa-

145

miliar with the U.S. system. This also aided the discussion. Her married name was Tsunekawa, but she became Iwata when she embarked on her career as a poet. At the time the author arrrived in Japan in 1981, she had been a highly respected faculty member at the United Nations Asia Far East Institute. She was very eager to be of assistance to the investigation, and her warmth and candidness in the interview provided the basis for an illuminating session.

First, the researcher pursued the matter of career patterns and geographical transfers of probation officers. "Yes," she noted, "those who pass the National Public Service Exam transfer more often than others, but there is still movement among the ranks of individuals who passed the lower level and middle level exams. People who pass the lower exam occasionally shift to another region of the country. Some of these people are indigenous to a local area, and of course they are not always eager to move, but they are encouraged to accept at least one or two moves during their careers." Asked about the nature of the various exams required to enter probation work, Iwata-san responded, "A candidate can choose among three exams and select certain subjects within each. For example, a person will take a general section like a general aptitude test, and then select a sub-exam from among categories like jurisprudence, sociology and social work, administrative sciences, or psychology." She continued, "While it's not generally known, there are some appointments made to probation officer positions in which individuals have not passed any exam; they are perhaps less then 10% of all those who enter."

Asked if clients were being rehabilitated in the system, she responded:

> We are making a modest impact. V.P.O.'s provide human contact and recidivism is perhaps around 30% now, if you just look at the shorter period of parole. But if you take a larger view and examine what happens over four or five years, recidivism rates will be closer to 40% or 50%. Of course, it depends on whether you include in your analysis those who were given a suspended sentence. Regarding juveniles, I once read a study that their rate was around 50%, if you include minor offenses. We are quite successful with adult parolees during the period they are under supervision, but that period is too short. Our parole system is too conservative. More than 80% are on parole for six months or less. We don't take enough risks with the system and it means, in

part, that we don't get access early enough to incarcerated offenders. Prison authorities are very selective about whom they release to us. The Parole Board could exercise discretion and select its own candidates but it does not. It acts passively in response to the prison authorities. Regulations are quite rigid here, more so than in the United States. My impression is that you have more freedom to fail in America. We have less, and if a mistake is made there is a great public outcry. Japanese society is quite conservative and agencies very bureaucratic.

Kyoko drew on the following data to support her view on recidivism rates during parole:

Adult Parole Terms - 1980	Recidivism Rate
less than 1 month	18.5%
less than 2 months	30.4%
less than 3 months	16.5%
less than 6 months	21.5%
less than 1 year	9.0%
less than 2 years	2.9%

On the subject of the strengths and weaknesses of the Volunteer Probation Officer system, she had this to say:

I can't say that professionals would be more successful in treatment or counseling, but I think the professionals are better at sizing up and evaluating client behavior. But, of course, it's difficult to say about volunteers—they vary. On the plus side we have the tradition that people can approach an older citizen and, as you know, most of the volunteers are older. Furthermore, the V.P.O.'s are indigenous to the area. Some do better than the professionals because of their life and work experiences. I admire those with a deep commitment to people, who are not authoritarian. They offer good human relationships. We can't tell if a volunteer is authoritarian during screening, its difficult to select out those types. A few, however, want to get social recognition for themselves. Those individuals I do not approve of—they're more concerned with themselves than with their clients. Screening of V.P.O.'s is vital, but since we don't have enough applicants we can't be selective. Also, we're competing with other volunteer services that may be more attractive to citizens. Our clients may visit or call a volunteer in the middle of the night or the police may call at night to a volunteer regarding his or her client. The older age cuts two ways. In rural, conservative areas, older people are looked up to, but then there is the problem of the generation gap. To influence people through brief human contact is very difficult, regardless of whether it's volunteers or professionals. In that context, peers, employers, and others exert an important influence in their human contacts. A brief contact is not a powerful instrument for change.

Some clients are very manipulative; they talk a good game. They may make frequent visits to a V.P.O.'s residence, but I know of cases where 'behind the curtain' they have committed serious criminal acts. Some volunteers are too kind and overlook too many things and that presents a different kind of problem.

Iwata-san was asked to comment on the halfway house system. She stated:

It's the people, because facilities are facilities. A question occasionally asked is would professionals do a better job in operating and staffing these hostels. In theory more use of professionals might help, but much really depends upon the personality of the individual. Perhaps some lawyers are better at relationships than caseworkers. The basic personality is more important than education or professional preparation.

Finally, she was asked to discuss the general attittude of Japanese citizens toward the rehabilitation of offenders.

Our problem is that probation and parole are not well known to the general public. These activities don't receive press coverage. My perspective can only be offered as a professional and academic. The academics may be more skeptical concerning whether rehabilitation works, but I think they are influenced by the Americans. We have always had criticism of the V.P.O. system. Ryuichi Hirano (a prominent Criminal Law professor at the University of Tokyo and later President) criticized the V.P.O. system a number of years ago and stated that our probation system is not standardized and professional (Iwata quoted from Hirano's book:). "Professional services may be good for some clientele, but not others. Therefore, we have to differentiate among our clientele. We should limit the followup to two or three years because too many other factors may enter after that." A different problem is that in urban society there is less respect for older probation officers and the clients chafe at having to disclose things to someone in their neighborhood. Confidentiality in reality is an illusion. For example, I had an instance in which the person was willing to make a long train ride (over an hour) to report to me directly because he did not want to visit the local V.P.O. and be observed by neighbors—everyone knows who the volunteers are.

An interview with Kazuo Yoshioka, a law professor at Kyoto University who had been interested in the halfway house movement, took an entirely different tact. "A policy dilemma exists," he noted, "because the Japanese system of hostels involves surveillance and help." He went on:

> a survey of residents of halfway houses indicated that some were unhappy with their ciurcumstances. Neighbors were also unreceptive, sensing that hostel residents might be dangerous. The objectives of hostels seems confused. Are they giving aid or preventing crime? Some of those surveyed had been able to adjust, but those residents believe that the state pays subsidies not to help them but to protect society from them. There was another case that is pertinent to our discussion. One resident of a hostel provided a stimulant to another person, a taxi cab driver, while in a hostel. The newspaper reporter's approach to the story was that all visitors to hostels should be checked—body searches—, by someone not in residence at the halfway house. If that were to occur, we would have another type of prison in existence. No, I think this matter ought to be approached differently. *The most important issue is that the ex-offender be perceived as a normal person* [author's italics]. By labeling them as ex-offenders, its almost impossible for them to live lives as normal persons. Also, the V.P.O.'s that run these houses and offer service to individual clients will disappear after a while. It's harder to recruit them than it used to be. My fundamental idea is to limit the role of the state in the life of a person.

A third interview with an outside scholar was conducted with Tadashi Moriyama of Waseda University in Tokyo. A young scholar, he identified his main professional interest as "public participation in criminal justice policy." Like Yoshioka, he philosophically seemed to favor less government intervention in community based programs for ex-offenders. For example, he commented:

> The hostels are under the aegis of the Minister of Justice and therefore the public perceives them as being associated with criminals and this perception is well established. These ex-offenders should be placed in facilities under the welfare agency to remove the stigma. If the facilities were private, though, the government probably wouldn't provide subsidies.

Asked about the possibilities of a system whereby each released offender would be given a grant to arrange his own housing, Moriyama replied, "I raised that point myself in a scholarly paper I published, and there were favorable comments from other academics."

Moriyama had been closely affiliated with the Koshinkai Rehabilitation Aid Hostel near Waseda University, one of the oldest hostels in Japan. Tadashi had outlined a number of areas in which private citizens might play a crucial role in the rehabilitation of offenders. First, private citizens could be mobilized to assist in supporting present government programs by directly helping hostel owners and by suporting the Volunteer Probation office movement. Secondly, the private sector might initiate its own halfway houses, but they would have to operate free from government regulation and without subsidies. Earlier in history there had been examples of these kinds of facilities. Thirdly, private citizens should act as watchdogs, monitoring activities of public prosecutors, being alert to heavy handedness and overreaching. These citizen groups would also be vigilant, for example, concerning the nonprosecution of white collar criminals. He noted that Japan does not have groups that support prisoners' rights, but that they exist in Europe and other countries. Fourthly, private citizens might take a more active role in resisting new government programs in the criminal justice field by blocking construction of new hostels, as they were already doing. Fifthly, Moriyama argued for greater efforts on the part of private citizens to engage in "self-protective" activities. It was his view that each individual ought to have the incentive to protect himself or herself from government sponsored programs.

Lessons for America

It has been the major purpose of this comparative study of Japan's community based programs for offenders to focus on and illluminate Japan's activities in this field. As the first major field study on this subject, the intent was to paint the broader landscape, contrasting Japan's activities with those of the United States. The task has proved challenging, given the vastly different cultural setting of each nation. Therefore, one has to be cautious about translating a successful project or program from one country to the other. Nonetheless, are there any lessons for America in what the Japanese are doing?

Overall, Japan appears to enjoy some greater degree of success than the United States in rehabilitating offenders. But it must be remembered that there are fewer offenders and many less violent ones. Recidivism rates are lower. Reflecting Japanese society generally, strong central government intervention is evident in the lives of offenders. As noted, all halfway houses are privately owned, although government controlled, leaving little room for private initiatives and experimental ventures. While a vast army of volunteers provide the day to day assistance to released offenders, their activities are closely monitored by the state. The "volunteers" are government appointed and dismissed.

Undeniably though, the system of volunteers has the virtue of being an inexpensive government budget item. The claim that volunteers ar better received by ex-offenders than professionals appears to be true, notwithstanding the criticism that some volunteers are too old and others are "medal seekers." Still, the overall results are positive. Ryōji Kawabata (1982), in a paper presented at the United Nations Far East Institute, cited a study that found that V.P.O.'s had a success rate of 80.6%, with just 19.4% of offenders under their supervision having recidivated. This is a lower rate of recidivism than figures offered by United States' officials in the handful of programs where data was available.

While there are limits to the impact of brief human encounters, as Kyoko Iwata observed, the one to one relationship offered by matchups between volunteers and ex-offenders in Japan appears to be superior to the typical parole situation in America whereby the large numbers of jurisdictions offer a variety of programs. True enough, thousands of American volunteers give their time and energy to these varied programs, but by virtue of the non-national nature of the system, organization suffers. Consequently, the idea of mobilizing vast numbers of private citizens to work with parolees in theory would appear to be a good one, but once again the difficulty must be confronted of organizing any national program in the United States in which the federal government has limited power. Such a program might serve as a model for other states, but it would still be problematical as to whether other states would adopt such a program. Perhaps there are too many conflicting interests involved, both political and individual, in our vast patchwork system of local, county, and state governments to be able to match the Japanese in this respect. Furthermore, and perhaps more importantly, the United States lacks the depth of commitment to volunteerism that exists in Japan.

A second area where one might consider borrowing from the Japanese is related to the subject of halfway houses. Japan's approach demonstrates that a creditable job can be undertaken by people who are not professionally trained. Although Japan does not staff their Rehabilitation Aid Hostels with former offenders, they rely on lay persons (often retired) not professional social workers, psychologists or psychiatrists. Kyoko Iwata is probably correct, the personality of the helper is more important than the educational background.

Many Japanese probation officials claim that their overall service is being seriously underfunded. Gradually, more halfway houses are closing because low subsidies, combined with decreasing accomodation rates, are forcing owners to cease operations. With crime continuing at a low rate, Japanese government officials seem to be unwilling to provide increased funding for rehabilitation programs. Nonetheless, those halfway houses surveyed in this study were attractive, comfortable facilities, with several offering newly renovated buildings. There is a sense that the Rehabilitation Bureau of the Ministry of Justice is a "step child" within the justice apparatus, but that's an impression the author developed. It receives proportionally less funding and lacks the political clout of other justice agencies.

Most Japanese citizens are ignorant of programs to rehabilitate offenders, but those that become aware of such efforts frequently fight them. Some new construction of hostels has encountered strong community resistance, preventing buildings from being erected. This lack of willingness to assist ex-offenders is, of course, not peculiar to Japan as was noted. Similar problems exist in Europe and the United States!

A third major consideration is the quasi-national nature of the system. As a result of this integrated system, the Japanese maintain national standards of entrance into the probation/parole field and effectively control policies and programs nationwide. Professional probation officers in all 47 prefectures must meet the same selection standards throughout. Partly, as a result, they are consistently a talented, bright group of professionals who are dedicated to their work. Since probation and parole are combined in Japan, certain economic benefits accrue from such a structure. In the U.S. they are separate functions and agencies.

By having a national program, the Japanese are able to offer an "elite" program for entrants, which provides a fast track for a handful of particularly bright college graduates. By rotating these elite around the country and through various types of work (supervision, research, aftercare, etc.) they train generalists just as they do in private industry. This helps in maintaining standardization. In summary, while certain benefits emerge from this quasinational system, it would be difficult for the U.S. to adopt, given our highly decentralized system of county, state, and federal services. As in so many instances, Americans eschew a central government model in favor of a decentralized one, even if the price is a less economical and less efficient apparatus.

One area where Japan seems to be lagging behind such countries as the United States, Great Britain, and the Netherlands, (particularly the latter two) is in the use of "community service." This is an alternative method of sentencing, whereby defendants can repay their debts to society through useful services to the community. Usually defendants asked to provide community service are low risk individuals. In the Netherlands, interviews the author conducted in 1985 with judges and probation officials indicated that defendants were required to engage in a specific number of hours per week beyond their regular employment so that it represented a sacrifice on the individual's part. It was being used increasingly for minor offenses.

The type of work performed varied tremendously from public health assistance, to work in a non-profit agency, to maintenance work in a national park. For example, in a national park a defendant might be asked to mow lawns, clean up debris, cut down underbrush or repair equipment.

A second area in which Japan is lagging behind the United States is inherent in its national system. Given its monolithic approach, there are a few experimental or innovative programs that are being explored. Over the long haul, this may hurt. The United States supports a much greater variety of programs.

In conclusion, there are no clear solutions to the United States's problem of how to rehabilitate offenders. Today, there is a limited effort being made to assist offenders re-entering the community, as most people feel that rehabilitation is an illusory ideal. A few bright spots exist, but there is no national effort underway in America at this time to try to enhance programs to rehabilitate offenders. Despite limited funding and a small cadre of professionals, the Japanese have found a way to maintain modest rates of recidivism—rates below those of the United States. The one to one relationship offered by the volunteer probation officer lies at the center of their system and is the most uniquely successful feature. Given the massive caseloads of American professionals, it is virtually impossible for us to provide assistance through a one to one relationship, although American volunteers make a small contribution. Finally, organization and professionalism are among the outstanding features of the Japanese approach. Their sense of pride in doing a good job was very much in evidence in this study of parole and community based programs for released offenders.

REFERENCES

Brennan, T. and Mason, L. "Community Service: A Developing Concept," *Federal Probation*, Volume 47, No. 2, June, 1983.

Kawabata, Ryōji. "Some Problems Relating to Halfway Houses." In *Resource Material Series No. 22*, United Nations Asia Far East Institute, Fuchu, Japan, December 1982, pp. 199–201.

Index